The Untied States of America

A Thinkable Alternative to Civil War II

The Untied States of America
A Thinkable Alternative to Civil War II

Fred Kilbourne

MILL CITY PRESS

Mill City Press, Inc.
2301 Lucien Way #415
Maitland, FL 32751
407.339.4217
www.millcitypublishing.net

Research by Brenda Cox and the author

Edited by Brenda Cox and the author

Formatted by Wendy Arakawa

Front cover by Kathleen Blum and Michael Lynch

Back cover photo by Alene Lynch

ISBN-13: 978-1-93640-046-1

Dedication

To my children and yours, and theirs.

The Author

Fred Kilbourne is an independent consulting actuary. His office is in San Diego.

Actuaries are mathematicians who specialize in identifying and projecting trends, and in finding ways to eliminate or minimize the adverse consequences of those trends.

Most actuaries concentrate on insurance programs or pension plans. Some consider issues outside these traditional fields of practice.

Credits

The primary source for much of the verbal information used to prepare this book was Wikipedia, the free encyclopedia (en.wikipedia.org). The scope and organization of this resource is a major aid to the modern author, who marvels at the diligence of his predecessors.

The primary source for much of the numerical information used to prepare this book was the privately-published 2018 Statistical Abstract of the United States, previously an annual publication of the US Census Bureau. The sources of the data remain federal or other government agencies.

Table of Contents

Chapter 1

Prologue

The purpose of this book is to promote thought and discussion about the previously unthinkable, a second civil war between the people of the United States of America.

The current division in the country, here early in the 21ˢᵗ Century, if projected using recent trends, is inconsistent with national unity in the near or distant future. This is not to say that improving national unity is impossible, merely that we're not headed in that direction. Alternative projection scenarios, each of which may be unlikely but nonetheless plausible, should be considered, if we are to reverse recent trends, and avert another civil war in the future of the United States of America.

Consider scenarios under which the country and the states stay together, more or less, but with national sovereignty diminished or eliminated. One such future would have the US yield to the United Nations for military, or economic, or political, or other, or all, matters of global or regional concern. For variations on this scenario replace "United Nations" with the World Trade Organization, or the Group of Eight or Eighty-Eight, or the European Union, or the Arab League, or a group of nations putting aside their differences to deny American hegemony. Any of these futures could come about by foreign invasion, military or otherwise, or by internal collapse, as by civil or incivil disobedience. They could come about suddenly (as by invasion following nuclear or biological attacks) or gradually (demographically, following persistent infiltration), or even democratically, (if the balance of political power stops teetering and shifts decisively to those favoring one side or the other). One or more of these projections may fail the plausibility test, but together they should not be dismissed in any brainstorming discussion of the likely future of the USA. They may be, however, even in combination, less likely than a future that includes Civil War II.

Our only Civil War to date is never thought of as Civil War I. But the term "World War I" was twin to "World War II", born on that same December day of 1941, before which it was called the Great War, or even the War to End All Wars. It's true that seven generations have come and gone with only one civil war in our history, but another is neither impossible nor implausible, and should not be unthinkable. Some may say that the increasing polarization and lack of civility in our national debate are signs of strength, of a healthy exchange of divergent views, of our mutual respect for freedom of expression. This comforting view is unavailable, however, to those who watch television, read newspapers, or listen to radio. The national debate is already a verbal war, with mutual respect and even civility among the early casualties. Divergent views are still freely expressed, but they reflect far less a spectrum of competing ideas than they do two opposing and warring camps of political slogans.

Furthermore, the trends are adverse and, ominously, the two camps are of roughly equal size, as can be seen by examining the early Presidential elections of the 21st Century. Violent eruptions have been increasing recently, but remain relatively sparse and minor, but so they were seven generations ago, before the attack on Fort Sumter that triggered Civil War I. We are well on our way to a repeat of that war, with one important difference – the oceans are no longer so vast as to protect us from those who would take advantage of our weakened condition during the war. And weakened we surely would be.

The divide between the two Americas is especially deep and enduring on the subject of race relations. Those on the left side of the divide assert that the problem persists because of racial discrimination by those on the right. Those on the right side counter that the problem is kept alive by those on the left for electoral advantage. African-Americans are to be found on both sides of the divide, but overwhelmingly on the left side. Most generally agree, however, and are joined by many white Americans, that race relations in the country are not good, and are not improving. Some propose reparations to black Americans for many years of slavery and, arguably, of racism. While no specific reparations proposal has yet gained much traction in public opinion, the concept persists and is not unthinkable. The time may be right for a mutually-advantageous reparations and racial self-determination program, such as presented herein, to be considered along with a regional self-determination program, also to be found in these pages.

The untying of the states of the USA will be said to be unthinkable. It may run counter to the thoughts and emotions of a lifetime, it may encounter ridicule or hostility, it may or may not advance the interests of all citizens – but it is thinkable. What's more, within the bedrock US Constitution, it's both speakable and potentially doable. Finally, it may well be an idea whose time has come, as the untenable and worsening national standoff vividly illustrates. Each side in the standoff hopes to unite the entire country in its own image, which is highly unlikely without terrible collateral damage.

This book was begun some years ago due to the author's perception that the country was headed toward another civil war. That perception is now more widespread, but still is shared by only a minority of the population. More people believe in the possibility or probability of other national disasters (e.g. economic collapse caused by escalating public debt, or environmental collapse caused by failure to remediate), however, some of which could be averted or ameliorated by a mutually agreeable breakup of the country along the lines suggested in this book. We no longer have the luxury of thinking that such things are unthinkable.

Abraham Lincoln had it right when he said "A house divided against itself cannot stand".

Chapter 2

The United States of America

<u>18th Century</u>

The 20 years between the 1763 and 1783 Treaties of Paris were momentous in terms of American independence from Great Britain. The 1763 Treaty ended the French and Indian War, but led to a series of Stamp Acts designed, effectively, to require the colonies to pay for the War and for the ensuing British military presence in North America. These were soon followed by the Townshend Acts, which added to the Stamp Act burdens imposed on the colonists, and which required the quartering of British soldiers in private homes. Public unrest resulted, leading to the 1770 Boston Massacre, in which taunted British troops fired on unarmed rioters, killing five men. The cycle of taxes, protests, and military response continued, culminating with the Boston Tea Party in 1773, which was in response to the Tea Act, but which directly led to the so-called Intolerable Acts. The colonists convened Continental Congresses in 1774 and 1775, resulting in the 1776 Declaration of Independence, meaning independence from Great Britain, and in 1777 in the creation of the Articles of Confederation and Perpetual Union of the United States of America. The British did not acquiesce, however, and the Revolutionary War was on, not formally to end until the Treaty of Paris in 1783. The Constitution of the United States of America was ratified in 1787, and became effective in 1789, at which time George Washington assumed his duties as the first President of the new confederation of thirteen in(ter)dependent states.

The path to the USA and its Constitution was tumultuous, with regional and local differences very much on display. The State of Franklin, for example, seceded from North Carolina, and applied for admission to the US. It was turned down in 1785, eventually becoming eight counties of the State of Tennessee, which had been a part of North Carolina, but which was admitted in its own right in 1796. The Republic of Vermont gave up its independence and in 1791 became the fourteenth state. Kentucky, which had previously been part of Virginia, became the fifteenth state the following year.

Among the many reasons for disputes among the states and regions of the US, the divisive issue of slavery was paramount. The Constitution (Article IV) required the return of escaped slaves to their owners, and the Fugitive Slave Act of 1793 put teeth into this provision. Opposition by Northern abolitionists led to reaction by Southern slaveholders, with both groups joined by many others from their respective regions. The Fugitive Slave Act of 1850 was one of many attempts at compromise, but its failure led in time to civil war.

19th Century

The key word for the new country during the 19th Century was "growth". The population grew from 5 million persons in 1800 to about 75 million in 1900. The number of African-Americans grew from under a million (nearly all slaves) at the beginning of the century, to about 4.5 million (about 90% slaves) in 1860, to nearly 9 million (no slaves) at the end of the century. The number of Native Americans dropped from about one million in 1800 to only about ¼ million in 1900. Growth in the gross national product (GNP, or the nearly equivalent GDP, the gross domestic product) was even more dramatic, from about $7 billion in 1800 to about $352 billion in 1900 (both amounts in constant 2000 dollars). Even the land itself grew, from under one million square miles at the beginning of the century to 3.6 million at the end, through purchases (Louisiana, Gadsden, Alaska) and the admission of 29 states (including Texas and California).

There was progress as well as growth in the US during the 19th Century. The country became smaller, in a sense, by the completion of the Erie Canal in 1825, the laying of a transatlantic cable in 1858, the establishment of the Pony Express in 1860, the joining of two lines making a transcontinental railroad in 1869, and the opening of the Brooklyn Bridge in 1883. The second war with Great Britain, in 1812, also led to US progress by contributing to the Second Industrial Revolution, whereby the republic was transformed from an agrarian society to an industrial powerhouse. Major American inventions of the century that facilitated this transformation included the cotton gin (actually, a 1794 invention), reaper, sewing machine, revolver, repeating rifle, oil well, barbed wire, subway, skyscraper, camera, telephone, and an improved incandescent lamp.

The greatest progress in the US during the 19th Century arguably was the elimination of "that peculiar institution" of slavery (offset somewhat by the concomitant near-elimination of the native American population). This progress came at great cost to the country, however, including over 600,000 military deaths (out of a population of 30 million) during the Civil War. The division between North and South (and within the West) over the issue of slavery deepened and hardened during the first six decades of the 19th Century, erupted during the Civil War, and persisted over subsequent issues for the remainder of the century, and beyond.

20th Century

Growth and progress continued to characterize the United States during the 20th Century. The population grew from 75 million to 282 million, with the number of African-Americans increasing from 9 million to 35 million and the number of Native Americans increasing from under ¼ million to nearly 2 million. The gross national product grew from $352 billion in 1900 to nearly $10 trillion in 2000 (both amounts in constant 2000 dollars). Americans continued their contributions to shrinking the world, from Robert Peary visiting the North Pole in 1909 to Charles Lindbergh flying across the Atlantic in 1927 to Neil Armstrong walking on the moon in 1969. The Industrial Revolution also continued in full force with the introduction of airplanes, motion pictures, and the mass production of automobiles; and with the development and use of the atomic bomb, computers, and the Internet.

US growth during the 20th Century was particularly pronounced for government. The cost of government at all levels, including both direct government spending and private costs incurred in complying with government mandates, went from 5% of GDP in 1900 to 50% in 2000. This was financed in part by taxation, including income taxation, which required the 16th Amendment to the Constitution. It was also financed in part by public debt, which grew from $60 billion in 1900 to $7 trillion in 2000 (both numbers in 2000 dollars). This acknowledged debt does not include the much-larger social insurance debt caused by Social Security and Medicare, nor does it include other "off-book" federal obligations.

There was only one US economic "Depression" in the 20th Century, but there were a number of wars. Wars during the century (with US deaths shown parenthetically) included World War I (116,708), World War II (407,316), Korea (36,914), Vietnam (58,169), Grenada (19), the Gulf War (269), and the so-called War on Terror (several thousand and counting). There was also a Cold War (with very few direct deaths) between the United States and the Soviet Union which lasted, in truth, if not in the public perception, from 1917 to 1989.

Civil rights were very much on the national agenda throughout the 20th Century, and were addressed by judicial decisions, legislation, and even by amendments to the Constitution. The 18th Amendment took away the right to drink alcoholic beverages, but the 21st Amendment restored that right. The 19th Amendment gave women the right to vote, the 24th forbade the use of poll taxes to restrict voting rights, and the 26th extended the right to vote to persons as young as 18. The Selective Service Acts of 1917 and 1940 imposed involuntary servitude by drafting young men into military service, with the draft not fully ended until 1973. President Franklin Roosevelt's Executive Order 9066 in 1942 resulted in the forced detention of more than 100,000 Japanese-Americans (mostly US citizens) in War Relocation Centers, and in the eventual payment by the government to these detainees of $20,000 per survivor in reparations. Judicial decisions also affected civil rights, including Brown v. Board of Education, concerning segregated education, and Roe v. Wade, concerning abortion.

Mixed progress and setbacks in race relations continued throughout the 20th Century in the United States. African-Americans joined the middle class in record numbers, and some achieved fame and fortune in various fields, but millions of other black people lived in communities where family dissolution, poverty, and crime were rampant. Federal

Civil Rights Acts (1957, 1960, 1964, and 1968) facilitated voting by black people and prohibited negative discrimination in education, housing, and employment, while affirmative action programs promoted discrimination favoring black people in some areas. Nonetheless, race riots escalated over those of previous centuries, including those in multiple cities during the so-called Red Summer of 1919 and following the assassination of Martin Luther King, Jr. in 1968. There were also major riots in Detroit in 1943 and 1967, in Los Angeles in 1965 and 1992, and in Newark in 1967, among others. The divide between the races was brought into sharp focus in 1995 when black football hero O. J. Simpson was acquitted by a mostly-black jury of the murder of two white people, and then subsequently was convicted by a mostly-white jury in a subsequent civil case. The Civil War of the 19th Century ended slavery in the United States, but more than a century later, relations between the races remained a source of ongoing conflict.

21st Century

The century in which we currently live is less than one-fifth over, but has already brought the country to a state of hostile division unmatched since the 1860's. The current century began with coordinated Islamist terrorist attacks on New York City and Washington, DC, using domestic commercial airplanes as improvised explosive devices, which served to introduce the suicide bomber to the American public. The death toll from these attacks totaled nearly 3000, which exceeded that of the only two other foreign attacks on US soil: Pearl Harbor (about 2400) and the War of 1812 (about 2300 combat deaths).

The country was briefly united after 9/11/01, but the fissure quickly appeared again in response to President George Bush's retaliatory and preventive incursions into Afghanistan and Iraq. Presidential candidate Barack Obama promised to increase American progress by expanding the role of government, and delivered significantly on that promise over the ensuing eight years. Presidential candidate Donald Trump in 2016 promised to "make America great again", and according to his supporters made significant progress on that promise in his early years as President, by working to undo the Obama legacy. Americans on the political left were horrified by this seeming reversal of their century of progress in expanding the role of the federal government, and

Americans not on the political left reacted accordingly. As these words are being written, (2018), the American political divide is profound, and getting worse by the day.

Chapter 3

The First Civil War

The central issue that led to the First Civil War (CWI) is generally conceded to have been slavery, although the South until recently used the term War Between the States to underscore the states' rights issue that also played a part. The two issues can be seen to be interwoven by considering the common thread of the word "freedom". The North wanted an end to slavery in order to fulfill the promise of freedom for all put forth by the Founding Fathers, notwithstanding that many of those early freedom-fighters were themselves slaveholders. The South wanted the country to remain a group of states that were united but not fused, in order to fulfill the promise of freedom from central government tyranny put forth by the Founding Fathers, most prominently in the Bill of Rights to the Constitution. The United States of America was not the first country to shed a great deal of its citizens' blood in an internal ideological debate, and it probably won't be the last. Furthermore, the debate goes on and, although the flow of blood has been largely staunched for over a century, the wound has not healed.

The freedom debate that led to CWI began many years before hostilities eventually flared into war. Negotiated settlements were reached on numerous occasions, only to be repudiated after a period of partial observance, generally to be replaced with shouting at a higher decibel level. Consider, for example, the following sentence from Article I of the US Constitution: "Representatives and direct Taxes shall be apportioned among the several States which may be included within this Union, according to their respective Numbers, which shall be determined by adding to the whole Number of free Persons, including those Bound to Service for a Term of Years, and excluding Indians not taxed, three fifths of all other Persons". Slavery was not even mentioned, at least not directly, in this obvious compromise between the parties.

As early as 1804, New Jersey became the *final* Northern state to enact legislation gradually abolishing slavery. Four years later Congress passed legislation banning the international slave trade, and attempted to enforce the ban by means of the US Navy. In 1816 the American Colonization Society was established for the purpose of sending freed slaves to Liberia, a new country set up in Africa for the purpose. In 1820 an important negotiated settlement, the Missouri Compromise, was enacted. This legislation admitted Maine to the Union as a free state, and Missouri as a slave state, with slavery restricted north of a rough extension of the Mason-Dixon line. The Compromise held, more or less, for more than a generation, but it also had the effect of marking the geographic divide between the two camps in the fight for the soul of United States of America.

The Compromise of 1850 admitted California as a free state and Utah as a slave state, established New Mexico as a slave territory, and included a strengthened fugitive slave law. Two years later the nation was reminded that the pen is mightier than the sword, with the publication by Harriet Beecher Stowe of *Uncle Tom's Cabin*. The debate escalated, along with its decibels, if not yet much violence. But the latter was soon to change.

In 1854 the Kansas-Nebraska Act effectively ended the Missouri Compromise by providing that popular sovereignty in the territories should decide all questions pertaining to slavery (states' rights), notwithstanding previous legislation restricting slavery in the North (slaves' rights). One result of the Act was the emergence of a new anti-slavery Republican Party, with Abraham Lincoln as one of its leaders.

Another result of the Kansas-Nebraska Act was an increase in political violence. The struggle between abolitionists and slaveholders to populate and control Kansas led to scattered but sustained violence, and to the apt term "Bleeding Kansas". The violence reached the nation's capitol when Southern Senator Preston Brooks severely injured, with his cane, Northern Senator Charles Sumner, on the floor of the US Senate. Several years later, but again not an unrelated event, John Brown attempted to ignite a slave rebellion in Virginia by attacking a federal armory at Harper's Ferry. His attempt failed, and he was hanged, but he also became a martyr to many in the North, and a warning to many in the South.

The country had become a tinderbox by 1860, although attempts at compromise continued throughout that year, and even beyond. The November election of Abraham Lincoln to be President led directly to secession by South Carolina the following month, and by six other states shortly thereafter. The April 12, 1861 attack on Fort Sumter, by the newly-formed Confederate States of America, was a foreseeable result of the unresolved freedom debate that had been going on for a century – and that persists to this day.

Slavery did not end in the United States by reason of the Emancipation Proclamation or during the War itself, although most slaves were freed as the Union Army occupied Confederate territory. Central government control over the states and their citizens, however, escalated quickly and considerably during the War, never to return to the low level envisioned by the Founding Fathers and realized for the first three generations of the new country. Lincoln's dedication to the preservation of the Union led him to adopt measures that would never have been allowed in antebellum America, and that were in some cases of dubious constitutionality. He blockaded the South without approval from Congress, suspended habeas corpus, and imprisoned thousands of suspected Southern sympathizers without trial. Congress also greatly expanded the power and resources of the federal government, issuing Treasury notes (Greenbacks) that weren't backed by gold, providing for unconstitutional income taxes, and enacting legislation that favored national banks over state banks. The most egregious exercise of federal power, however, was the imposition of the draft, which is arguably a form of slavery that is temporary but often fatal.

Chapter 4

The Interwar Period

Reconstruction following the War (1865-1877) put an end to the slavery issue in the freedom debate, but merely stoked the fires of the central government control issue. Three Reconstruction Amendments to the Constitution were enacted during the five years immediately following Civil War I (CWI). Amendment XIII outlawed slavery throughout the land. Amendment XIV had several parts, including removal of the "three fifths of all other Persons" provision of Article I, barring from public office persons who had violated their oath to uphold the US Constitution, and forbidding questioning the validity of the public debt of the United States (notwithstanding that Amendment I says that "... Congress shall make no law...abridging the freedom of speech..."). Amendment XV disallowed voting restrictions based on "race, color, or previous condition of servitude..." – but was widely ignored, awaiting subsequent civil rights legislation.

In addition to the foregoing Constitutional amendments, at least eight Civil Rights Acts were passed by Congress from the end of CWI to the dawn of the 21st Century:

- 1866 – All persons born in the United States, "excluding Indians not taxed", are citizens "without regard to any previous condition of slavery or involuntary servitude". Racial discrimination in housing or employment was forbidden, although enforcement was largely deferred until the civil rights movement of the 20th Century.

- 1871 – This Act was popularly known as the Ku Klux Klan Act, and was used by federal officials during Reconstruction to decimate (temporarily) the Klan. Its other provisions, such as protection against unreasonable search and seizure, similarly were largely deferred until the civil rights movement of the next Century.

- 1875 – All persons, regardless of race or previous condition of slavery, are entitled to the same treatment in "public accommodations". This Act was subsequently found to be unconstitutional, but its provisions largely became law by means of 20th Century civil rights legislation.

- 1957 – This Act established the Civil Rights Commission, but was largely ineffective in its voting rights goals.

- 1960 – This voting rights legislation was signed into law by President Eisenhower after the longest Senate filibuster in history, by 18 Southern Democrats, finally ended.

- 1964 – Segregation in schools and public places is outlawed, and discrimination based on race in government and employment is banned. The Act also established the Equal Employment Opportunity Commission.

- 1968 – Also known as the Fair Housing Act, this law basically provided for enforcement of the housing provisions of the Civil Rights Act of 1866.

- 1991 – This Act expanded the civil rights of employees who claim discrimination by their employers, providing for jury trials and limited general damage awards.

Civil rights legislation since CWI is a clear manifestation of the ongoing freedom debate in the country. Such legislation is by definition intended to enhance individual freedom, by countering legal and social limits on the full emancipation of former slaves, and their descendants.

It also curbs states' rights, at least to the extent those rights conflict with federal laws or court decisions. It is less clear as a delineator between the two sides in the build-up to a second Civil War (CWII). The first three major civil rights acts were spearheaded by Republicans, during Reconstruction; the next two again by Republicans; and the 1964 Act by Northern Democrats with considerable support from Republicans, over the vigorous objections of Southern Democrats. The two Parties have changed significantly over time, of course, and "the two sides in the build-up" are imperfectly represented by Democrats and Republicans. It is fair to say in general, however, that Democrats continue the cause of the abolitionists, working to expand freedom (from social as well as legal constraints) to slave descendants and to members of other "oppressed" groups – while at the same time working to move power from states and individuals to the central government. Republicans, on the other hand, continue the cause of the Founding Fathers, working to resist the seemingly inexorable shift of power to that central government (in this, they are fairly called reactionaries) – while at the same time usually supporting states' rights that are sometimes at the expense of individual freedom. Among the many ironies of history are the facts that Founding Father George Washington was a slaveholder and abolitionist Abraham Lincoln was a Republican. Civil rights legislation has followed a tortuous and uneven road in the interwar period, but the freedom debate goes on.

Consider the dozen amendments to the US Constitution that were passed in the 20th Century. Two clearly increased the power of the central government: XVI, permitting federal income taxation, and XVIII, prohibiting the manufacture, sale, or transportation of alcoholic beverages. Three expanded individual freedom by extending the right to vote to women (XIX), citizens of the District of Columbia (XXIII), and those 18 through 20 years of age (XXVI). Two others clearly advanced individual freedom: XXI, repealing Prohibition, and XXIV, forbidding poll taxes (although this was also a states' rights issue). The other five amendments were substantially internal to government (such as XXII, which limits the President to two terms of office).

While all this was going on in Washington, Americans were busy with other activities as well:

- <u>Reactions to Reconstruction</u> – The legacy of CWI and subsequent Reconstruction (1863-77) is still being debated, but several things are clear from the record. Presidential Reconstruction (1863-66) under Lincoln and Johnson was firm on the abolition of slavery, but its goal was national reconciliation and re-admittance of Southern states to the Union. Congressional Reconstruction (1866-73) had as its goal voting and other civil rights for freedmen, but also was directed at punishment of the South. During the subsequent Redemption (1873-77), white Southerners reasserted a degree of control over their states, and over the so-called freedmen, culminating with the end of Reconstruction following the brokered Presidential election of 1876.

- <u>Indians and Native Americans</u> – As was noted above, the number of Indians in the country was reduced by 75% during the 19th Century (to about 250,000 in 1900), and was then increased by 700% during the 20th Century (to about two million Native Americans in 2000). The earlier century was characterized by armed conflict (with some Indian victories, such as at Little Bighorn in 1876, but with more losses, such as at Wounded Knee in 1890) and the relocation of survivors onto reservations. The latter century was characterized by increased civil rights for Native Americans, highlighted by the Indian Citizenship Act of 1924. At the end of the 20th Century, Native Americans were plaintiffs in a class action lawsuit alleging mismanagement of American Indian money by the US government, with a 2007 settlement offer of $7 billion rejected as mere "pennies on the dollar". Although the term "reparations" is seldom used in connection with Native American claims, the Indian Gaming Regulatory Act of 1988 led to an industry that now has gross revenues of about $20 billion annually, with net revenues going to nearly half of the 562 federally-recognized tribes in the country, and with funding provided disproportionately by lower-income Americans.

- <u>Progress and Growth</u> – It should not be thought that the United States were idle during the many years since Civil War I. Social progress (and setbacks) and other activities of Americans and their government(s) are sketched above and below. Medical and other technological advances were dramatic, profoundly affecting the lives of all. Polio and smallpox were eradicated, other infectious diseases were diminished, and diseased or injured body parts became replaceable. People and knowledge became more accessible with inventions ranging from the telephone (1876) to radio (1920) to the Internet (circa 1990). Atomic power was harnessed for the purposes of blowing up people and buildings (1945) and of providing energy needed by electric light bulbs (1879) and subsequent inventions. People became more mobile as a result of inventions such as the airplane (1903) and the automobile assembly line (1908), and the world shrank as a result of explorers such as Charles Lindbergh (1927) and Neil Armstrong (1969). The country itself grew, notably with the addition of Alaska and Hawaii as states (1959). The population grew even more dramatically, under the triple influence of births, immigration, and greatly reduced mortality rates. But the most dramatic growth of all was in government.

- <u>Growth of the Government</u> – The tremendous growth in the cost and power of the federal government during CWI has been noted. This subsided substantially immediately following that war, and at the dawn of the 20th Century the total cost of government at all levels was about 5% of the gross national product. This includes the cost of compliance with regulations, but does not include the cost of future government payments (e.g. Social Security and Medicare). The success of the government advocates during the 20th Century can be seen not only in the civil rights legislation that was passed, but also in the fact that the cost of government grew to about 50% of GNP by the dawn of the 21st Century. Major increases in the economic power of the US government took place during the presidencies of Woodrow Wilson (Federal Reserve, Internal Revenue Service), Franklin Roosevelt (numerous federal agencies, Social Security), and

Lyndon Johnson (Medicare, Medicaid) – all Democrats. Young men were forced into military service and Japanese-Americans were interned into camps – again at the hands of Democratic Presidents. The USA avoided one supranational organization, the League of Nations, but joined another, the United Nations – again both promoted by Democratic Presidents. Judicial decisions advanced civil liberties (Brown v. Board of Education, Roe v. Wade), but at the expense of already declining states' rights. Any credit due the federal government, however, must be tempered by its spectacular fiscal irresponsibility, which is increasingly emulated by the public (the national savings rate has dropped greatly over the past five decades). The Federal Reserve inherited a dollar that, though sometimes volatile, had roughly maintained its value over the five generations from the founding of the country to the founding of the Fed, and has replaced it with a dollar that is now worth less than a nickel. Further, the excess of promises over provision, particularly in federal entitlement programs, now exceeds several years of gross national product – on a present value basis (i.e. the amount of money that would need to be invested *now* to meet the *excesses*, not the promises, as they come due). The symbol of America may be the eagle, but that whoosh of feathers is chickens coming home to roost.

- <u>Wars, Hot and Cold</u> – The interwar period between the Civil Wars has been lengthy, but it has not been free from conflict with outsiders. The Cold War between the USA and the USSR lasted over 40 years, but was really neither war nor peace. The longest period of peace (apart from the Indian Wars) was the 33 years from the end of CWI to the Spanish-American War. There followed a war for each generation (19 years to WWI, then 23 years to WWII), after which the pace picked up (only 5 years to the Korean War, and 11 more to the Vietnam War). Apart from relatively minor skirmishes (fewer than 300 US servicemen killed in the Grenada Invasion and Persian Gulf War combined) it was then nearly 30 years until the country engaged radical Islam in a war that may well exceed the combined durations, if not casualties, of all previous US wars. Public reactions to the wars against communism and terrorism don't fit neatly into the abolitionist/states' rights conflict of CWI, but the polarization has been profound, and has followed rather faithfully the regional separations depicted on the cover of this book.

- <u>Domestic Violence</u> – The relative dangers of different vocations are often debated, but it is seldom recognized that the most dangerous job of all is to be President of the United States of America. (That does lead to the question as to why the Presidency is also the most sought-after job in the country, with the discouraging answer being that the power of the job makes the risk worthwhile to some). The mortality rate from assassination alone is nearly 2% per year (there were successful assassination attempts in 1863, 1881, 1901, and 1963), not to mention 14 failed assassination attempts (12 in the 20th Century), and at least one murder of a prominent Presidential candidate (1968). In spite of this record, however, the period following our civil war has been relatively peaceful at home. Recent homicide rates have been about 5 per 100,000 population in the United States, which is well below our neighbor Mexico (19) and other Latin American countries such as Brazil (30) and Venezuela (56) – not to mention countries that didn't report murder rates at all to the World Health Organization, such as the entire continent of Africa – although the US is admittedly higher than such relatively safe places as Japan and Switzerland, both of which have murder rates less than one-tenth of the US rate. The recent US homicide rate is about half the prevailing rate over the preceding generation, but is in line with the average rate over the first several generations of the 20th Century. Another measure of domestic violence is riots, with the United States again ranked favorably on the world stage, if not among the most peaceful countries. US riots have had various causes, such as opposition to the draft (New York City, 1863), but most of the 19th Century riots were directed at specific groups: Catholics (Philadelphia, 1844), Germans (Louisville, 1855), Chinese (Los Angeles, 1871), or Italians (New Orleans, 1891). There were a number of riots during the so-called Red Summer of 1919 but, although nominally directed at Bolsheviks, the real targets in the main were black Americans. Subsequent race riots, however, have generally been instigated by blacks, notably the Watts riots in Los Angeles (1965), those in Detroit and Newark (1967), those in a number of cities following the assassination of Martin Luther King, Jr. (1968), and again in Los Angeles (1992) following the videotaped beating of Rodney King.

The United States of America cannot fairly be called either violent or peaceful, without major qualification. Like nearly all of its citizens, including the most violent, as well as those of other countries, it is peaceful almost all of the time. Furthermore, it is slow to anger, or at least to acting on that anger, erupting in violence only when a long-simmering injustice (slavery or, from a different point of view, interference in states' rights) is ignited by a triggering event (firing on Fort Sumter, for example, or the election of Abraham Lincoln). Once the bomb has gone off, however, it is devilishly difficult to put the pieces back together again. Civil War I did yield one great benefit (an end to slavery), but its costs were horrendous at the time (death and destruction) and subsequently (unbridled power to the central government), and it did not result in a house that is undivided, by region or race. Civil War II, if it is not avoided, cannot be better.

Chapter 5

The Second Civil War

It is understandable that it has been until recently unthinkable that the United States of America could ever find itself in another civil war. The only such war this country ever had was many years ago, and the outcome seemed to ensure that the states would stay united forever, and that there would be no more talk of secession. Furthermore, the violence that is a necessary ingredient of a civil war has been largely confined to attacks on individuals by other individuals, or from time to time by one group (Ku Klux Klan) or another (Black Panthers) or even by the government against individuals (drug busts) or groups (Branch Davidians). No states have either attacked their neighbors or, until recently, threatened secession, and the federal government has been so ascendant since the days of Lincoln that it has not needed overt violence to have its way (e.g. the judicial repeal by stealth of the tenth amendment to the Constitution). But "unthinkable" is no synonym for "impossible", and indeed it can be argued that the failure to even contemplate a future event adds to the probability that it will come to pass.

A useful way to think about the future is to postulate various plausible scenarios, and then to try to determine the likelihood of each. Further thinking on the topic may investigate ways by which a given scenario can be avoided, or at least influenced to maximize its benefits or minimize its damage. Various scenarios were set forth in Chapter 1, all of which shared a vision of a country that stayed together in spite of reduced national sovereignty. Chapter 9 considers alternative political scenarios, called prognoses. Other scenarios are plausible, of course, including some that see the United States truly uniting in the face of some external threat. Radical Islam appeared to most to be such in the final months of 2001, and the country did unite, in the main, for a brief time. China could pose such a threat in the not-distant future, whether economically or militarily or both. Scenarios can also be imagined under which threats subside and opportunities grow, and our national debate moderates its tone and becomes mere background noise as US citizens go about their lives. The future is not necessarily a terrible place. The horizon doesn't have to be the end of the world.

The United States are unlikely to untie voluntarily unless faced with imminent civil war. The point of this book is to call attention to trends that are headed in that disturbing direction, and to suggest a thinkable alternative to merely riding the trends to see where they take us. Herewith are several scenarios, each of which has been constructed to be at least minimally plausible, and to culminate with the Second Civil War.

Scenario #1

The retirement of the aging Baby Boomers proves to gobble up an even larger portion of the federal budget than was anticipated at the opening of the century. This is partly due to reduced federal income because of an economy that itself has been reduced in response to environmental and other regulations, among other causes. The federal government and the so-called blue states (liberal) are loath to relax the regulations on the grounds that, while we may have impoverished our children, we must not leave them a planet that is uninhabitable. The so-called red states (conservative) counter that these regulations are creating escalating hardships for their citizens and that, in any event, they are ineffectual in achieving their stated purpose. Alaska is in particularly dire straits, in that it is uniquely dependent on oil to heat the homes in the state and to transport food to the tables of its people. Accordingly, and in direct contravention of federal laws and regulations, Alaska decides to go after North Slope oil, and to keep it for themselves. The federal government mobilizes its military forces, and makes plans to invade Alaska to enforce the law. Red states such as West Virginia, however, see Alaska as a forewarning of their future, and resist the passage of federal troops through their territory. A group of Mountain

State soldiers not only refuses to be deployed for the campaign to force Alaska to submit, but sabotages their unit's ordnance as well. Civil War II follows just as Gettysburg followed Fort Sumter.

Scenario #2

Radical Islam finally drops the other shoe, with a second coordinated attack on New York City that dwarfs that of long-ago and mostly-forgotten September 11, 2001. First is a low-yield nuclear explosion that kills about 75,000 people outright, with as many more expected to die subsequently due to blunt trauma or radiation disease. Second is the emergence shortly thereafter of an outbreak of smallpox, with casualties that exceed those of the bomb. The bomb is determined to have been in a cargo container, and forensic analysis leads to the conclusion, with moderately high certainty, that it originated in an Iranian nuclear facility. The smallpox virus almost certainly came from supplies maintained but inadequately controlled by Russia or the United States, with distribution by ISIS at several City locations on the day the bomb was exploded. Since ISIS is widely dispersed, with no country known with certainty to give safe haven to its members, there is only minority public support for retaliation against Muslim countries such as Pakistan. Such is not the case with Iran, however, with a majority of the US public demanding nuclear attacks on that country. A sizeable minority, on the other hand, including a significant majority of federal policymakers, argues against such retaliation, both on the grounds of uncertainty that the Iranian government instigated the attack, and also on the grounds that many innocent Iranian civilians would be killed and that the specter of a Holy War would be raised. The ensuing debate quickly escalates into violence, at first in the form of an insurrection against Washington, the seat of federal power, but soon thereafter fracturing the country as the sides are drawn for the battles of Civil War II.

Scenario #3

The federal government chooses to default on some Treasury bonds rather than to further exacerbate the escalating inflation that has wreaked havoc on the US economy. An attempt is made to limit the damage by targeting bonds held by a few extremely wealthy persons, most of whom sign a petition justifying and supporting the default. The result is catastrophic, however, as the market for all Treasuries collapses, runs on banks become widespread, and recession sinks into a profound economic depression. Food joins medical care in being rationed, with severe penalties for participating in the inevitable black market. Rural areas nonetheless remain adequately fed and the suburbs remain orderly, but tensions rise in the cities. Obesity shrinks as a national health problem, but it is observed that government workers and others with political influence continue to fill out their clothes. Food riots break out in some inner cities, and threaten to spread. The political response, justified as affirmative action, is to adjust the rationing rules so as to move additional food into the inner cities. This provokes truly widespread food riots, with the rioters made up of the millions who qualify for neither affirmative action nor political favors. The population splits on the basis of this and other grievances, and Civil War II is underway.

None of these or other scenarios are inevitable. There is another and better way to the future, set forth in the following chapter.

Chapter 6

The *Untied* States of America

There is precedent for the Untied States of America, of course, going back to the 18th Century Articles of Confederation (and Perpetual Union), under which the individual states retained most elements of nationhood and yet were bound together in a specified confederation. A modern-day counterpart is the pre-Brexit European Union, a confederation of interdependent states with a fairly strong central government. The proposed new-USA has at least three layers of government (confederation, land, state) and may have many more (county, city, water district, etc.). Only one of these layers is new (land), although that government (e.g. Progressiveland) will be the one that is recognized as a country on the world stage (and presumably in the United Nations, for those lands that choose to apply for membership in that body). The proposed confederation government (see Chapter 8) is but a pale shadow of the former United States of America government, confined substantially to managing the untying of the states and the national reparations plan (see Chapter 7), and to mediating issues that arise among the lands of the new-USA.

It is important to the transition, if not to the ultimate success of the venture, that the untying of the states of America be done in accordance with the rule of law. It should be left to legal scholars and the political process to determine whether this untying can only be accomplished by replacing the existing Constitution, or whether the wisdom of the Framers was great enough that the proposed restructuring of the old-USA can be realized by means of one or more amendments. In either event, there needs to be (with a nod, if not an apology, to Thomas Jefferson) a declaration of the causes which impel the separation of the proposed lands from one another and from the central deity (DC) that has inflicted "repeated injuries and usurpations" on its subjects. This is not the first time in history that it has become necessary for people to dissolve the "political bands which have connected them with one another", and to institute new government that will permit them to "assume among the powers of the earth" the separate and equal station to which they are entitled. The bill of particulars against the federal government is lengthy, but can be illustrated with a few examples. DC has erected a multitude of new offices, and has sent hither swarms of officers to harass the people, and to eat out their substance. DC has affected to render the military independent of and superior to the civil power, and has kept among us, in times of peace, "standing armies without the consent of our legislatures". DC has conspired to facilitate the judicial repeal of the tenth amendment of the US Constitution, which states that the powers not delegated to DC by the Constitution, nor prohibited by it to the states, are reserved to the states respectively, or to the people. The untying of the US states is amply justified, and can be done legally and without violence.

The proposed nine lands set forth in this chapter were prompted by the fact, coincidental or not, that the results of the first five Presidential elections of the 21st Century starkly illustrated the regional nature of the profound political divide in the country. The first four election results differed only in relatively minor ways, and even the surprising 2016 election results don't dramatically undermine the regional divide shown on the cover. In future elections it is very likely that very large minorities of the population will be extremely unhappy with their prospects under the old 50-state structure. Furthermore, and central to our thesis, most of these unhappy citizens live in states and regions where a majority of their neighbors share their unhappiness. This unhappy state of affairs can be alleviated by untying the 50 states and recombining them into groups of states with relatively common interests and perspectives, especially with regard to the appropriate role of government, and especially the federal government. The process will begin with consideration and discussion of the concept, along the lines proposed in these pages, and will proceed along a path that defies prediction, but that will likely include a Convention of the States (see www.conventionofstates.com), as provided by the Constitution. The reparations concept, also proposed in these pages, seems unlikely to be realized except by means of the Constitutional Convention, but it could well serve as a catalyst or facilitator in that connection.

The nine pages that follow present in tabular form the regional divide in the country, and support the division proposal that is shown on the cover of the book. The tables and text also show clearly that each new land is viable by pertinent measures, with comparably-sized countries shown for support. For example, the new Appalachialand has approximately the same population as Venezuela, the same area as Spain, and the same GDP as Canada.

The Appendices present further data to support the assertion that the proposed new lands should be well able to take their places among the world's nations.

6A – PROGRESSIVELAND

The eleven states (plus the District of Columbia) that make up Progressiveland comprise the most liberal region of the country. Indeed, they may choose to call themselves Liberalland, a name that would be distasteful to relatively few of their citizens. This new land, about the size of Spain, will be a powerhouse among nations, with a population nearly that of the United Kingdom and a gross domestic product midway between that of Germany and Japan. Its foreign policy will be characterized by negotiation over confrontation, and it will have particularly good relations with the European Union. It will have a broad national health insurance plan, and abortion and gay rights will be secure. Gun control legislation will be passed without the constraints of the erstwhile Second Amendment. Presidential candidates may include Bernie Sanders and Elizabeth Warren.

ST	PTY	ELEC	POP	GDP	AREA	COAST
CT	D	7	3.6	263	5	618
DE	D	3	1.0	70	2	381
DC	D	3	0.7	127	0	0
MA	D	11	6.8	508	8	1519
MD	D	10	6.0	378	10	3190
ME	D	3	1.3	59	31	3478
NH	D	4	1.3	78	9	131
NJ	D	14	8.9	581	7	1792
NY	D	29	19.7	1488	47	1850
PA	R	20	12.8	725	45	89
RI	D	4	1.1	57	1	384
VT	D	3	0.6	31	9	0
PROG	12	111	63.8	4365	174	13432

See next page for table notes.

ST – state postal code
PTY – winning party in 2016 election
ELEC – electoral votes received by winning party (2016)
POP – population (millions) UK-65
GDP – gross domestic product (billion dollars) Japan-4949
AREA – land area (1000 square miles) Spain-193
COAST – coastline (statute miles)

PROG – Progressiveland

6B – DIXIELAND

The seven states that make up Dixieland comprise the most conservative and least liberal region of the new-USA. An alternative name might be Southland. This new land, about the size of Nigeria, will also be a powerhouse, with a population about that of Italy and a gross domestic product larger than that of the United Kingdom. Its foreign policy will be characterized by negotiation, but only from a position of strength. It will permit broad economic freedom within its borders, but it will not be fairly described as a libertarian nation. The social agenda of religious conservatives will generally prevail, with substantial limits on abortion and with gay marriage being illegal. Legal immigration will be limited and the borders of the land will be secured. Presidential candidates may include Marco Rubio and Rick Scott.

ST	PTY	ELEC	POP	GDP	AREA	COAST
AL	R	9	4.9	205	51	607
FL	R	29	20.6	927	54	8426
GA	R	16	10.3	525	58	2344
MS	R	6	3.0	108	47	359
NC	R	15	10.1	518	49	3375
SC	R	9	5.0	210	30	2876
VA	D	13	8.4	494	39	3315
DIXIE	7	97	62.3	2987	328	21302

ST – state postal code
PTY – winning party in 2016 election
ELEC – electoral votes received by winning party (2016)
POP – population (millions) Italy-62
GDP – gross domestic product (billion dollars) United Kingdom-2651
AREA – land area (1000 square miles) Nigeria–352
COAST – coastline (statute miles)

DIXIE – Dixieland

6C – APPALACHIALAND

The five states that make up Appalachialand comprise a group of states that tend conservative but that were often in play in recent national elections (unlike, say, Massachusetts and South Carolina). This new land, nearly the size of Spain, will also be a major country, with a population equal to that of Venezuela and a gross domestic product similar to that of Canada. Its foreign policy will also be characterized by negotiation, but again only from a position of strength. It will permit substantial but not unlimited economic freedom within its borders, and the social agenda of religious conservatives will generally prevail, but not to the extent found in Dixieland. Legal immigration will be limited and the borders of the country will be secured. Presidential candidates may include John Kasich and Rand Paul.

ST	PTY	ELEC	POP	GSP	AREA	COAST
IN	R	11	6.6	342	36	0
KY	R	8	4.4	197	39	0
OH	R	18	11.6	626	41	0
TN	R	11	6.7	329	41	0
WV	R	5	1.8	73	24	0
APPAL	5	53	31.1	1567	181	0

ST – state postal code
PTY – winning party in 2016 election
ELEC – electoral votes received by winning party (2016)
POP – population (millions) Venezuela–31
GDP – gross domestic product (billion dollars) Canada–1536
AREA – land area (1000 square miles) Spain–193
COAST – coastline (statute miles)

APPAL – Appalachialand

6D –UNIONLAND

The four states that make up Unionland comprise a region that is generally liberal, but which was a major agent of change in the 2016 election. An alternative name might be Laborland. This new land, about the size of France, will be nearly the equal of Canada in terms of population and slightly greater than Italy in terms of economic output. Its foreign policy will be consistent with that of the Northeast region/land, but it will be more nationalistic and less quick to negotiate. It may have a limited national health insurance plan, but abortion and gay rights will be negotiated within the national legislature. School vouchers and right-to-work laws will be vigorously debated in Unionland. Presidential candidates may include Keith Ellison and Scott Walker.

ST	PTY	ELEC	POP	GDP	AREA	COAST
IL	D	20	12.8	792	56	0
MI	R	16	9.9	487	57	0
MN	D	10	5.5	335	80	0
WI	R	10	5.8	310	54	0
UNION	4	56	34.0	1924	247	0

ST – state postal code
PTY – winning party in 2016 election
ELEC – electoral votes received by winning party (2016)
POP – population (millions) Canada–36
GDP – gross domestic product (billion dollars) Italy–1859
AREA – land area (1000 square miles) France–247
COAST – coastline (statute miles)

UNION–Unionland

6E – HEARTLAND

The ten states that make up Heartland comprise a region that is generally conservative, but less religious than the Southeast and less libertarian than the Mountain States. An alternative name might be Farmland. This new land, about the size of Saudi Arabia, will have a population the size of South Africa and a GDP larger than that of the United Kingdom. With Texas contributing over half of that economic output, the voice of that state will be loud in matters such as foreign policy, but the other nine states may be expected to turn down the volume somewhat, depending on the extent to which minority states' rights are protected in Heartland politics. Farm policy will be paramount in the new land, and food exports will be a cornerstone of the economy. Presidential candidates may include Ted Cruz and Gregg Abbott.

ST	PTY	ELEC	POP	GDP	AREA	COAST
AR	R	6	3.0	121	52	0
IA	R	6	3.1	179	56	0
KS	R	6	2.9	153	82	0
LA	R	8	4.7	235	43	7721
MO	R	10	6.1	301	69	0
ND	R	3	0.8	52	69	0
NE	R	5	1.9	115	77	0
OK	R	7	3.9	183	69	0
SD	R	3	0.9	48	76	0
TX	R	36	27.9	1617	261	3359
HEART	10	90	55.2	3004	854	11080

ST – state postal code
PTY – winning party in 2016 election
ELEC – electoral votes received by winning party (2016)
POP – population (millions) South Africa–55
GDP – gross domestic product (billion dollars) United Kingdom–2651
AREA – land area (1000 square miles) Saudi Arabia–830
COAST – coastline (statute miles)

HEART–Heartland

6F – ROCKYLAND

The nine states that make up Rockyland comprise a region that is relatively conservative, but with a strong libertarian streak. An alternative name might be Mountainland. This new land, substantially larger than India, will have a similar sized population to that of Taiwan, and an economy almost that of Spain. It will be second only to Heartland in oil and natural gas production, and may turn out to be first in potential energy production. Its foreign policy won't be isolationist, but it will be less quick to engage other countries in disputes than some of the other lands. Presidential candidates may include Mike Lee and Susana Martinez.

ST	PTY	ELEC	POP	GDP	AREA	COAST
AK	R	3	0.7	51	571	33904
AZ	R	11	6.9	303	114	0
CO	D	9	5.5	324	104	0
ID	R	4	1.7	67	83	0
MT	R	3	1.0	46	146	0
NM	D	5	2.1	93	121	0
NV	D	6	2.9	148	110	0
UT	R	6	3.1	156	82	0
WY	R	3	0.6	38	97	0
ROCKY	9	50	24.5	1226	1428	33904

ST – state postal code
PTY – winning party in 2016 election
ELEC – electoral votes received by winning party (2016)
POP – population (millions) Taiwan–24
GDP – gross domestic product (billion dollars) Spain–1237
AREA – land area (1000 square miles) India–1148
COAST – coastline (statute miles)

ROCKY–Rockyland

6G – GREENLAND

The two states that make up Greenland comprise a region that is generally liberal, but with an emphasis on environmental concerns. Hence its name, which is also the name of a Danish island which is very large (about the size of Heartland), but which is not a country, which has a population less than 1% that of our subject region/land, and which has no known nuclear weapons. An alternative name might be Woodland. This new land, the same size as Iraq, will have a population equal to that of Belgium, and an economy about the same size as Switzerland. Its foreign policy will be generally accommodating, except when it comes to matters of the environment such as global warming and drilling for oil. It will offer rather more economic freedom than Progressiveland, but its public lands will be expanded and subject to greater protection. Presidential candidates may include Patty Murray and Ron Wyden.

ST	PTY	ELEC	POP	GDP	AREA	COAST
OR	D	7	4.1	227	96	1410
WA	D	8	7.3	470	66	3026
GREEN	2	15	11.4	697	162	4436

ST – state postal code
PTY – winning party in 2016 election
ELEC – electoral votes received by winning party (2016)
POP – population (millions) Belgium–11
GDP – gross domestic product (billion dollars) Switzerland–669
AREA – land area (1000 square miles) Iraq–169
COAST – coastline (statute miles)

GREEN–Greenland

6H – PROMISEDLAND

The single state that makes up Promisedland comprises a region that has historically been liberal with a libertarian streak, but which in recent years has trended ever more strongly to the left. It alone among the new lands may expect major changes in its demographics (see Chapter 7), which makes prognostications as to its characteristics relatively uncertain. An alternative name might be Kingland. Nearly the size in area and population of Iraq, its GDP will be about that of the United Kingdom. Its foreign policy will probably be assertive, especially concerning environmental issues such as global warming, subject to constraints imposed by the United Nations (of which it will surely be a member). Its domestic policies remain to be seen. Presidential candidates may include Barack Obama and Kamela Harris.

ST	PTY	ELEC	POP	GDP	AREA	COAST
CA	D	55	39.3	2603	156	3427
PROM	1	55	39.3	2603	156	3427

ST – state postal code
PTY – winning party in 2016 election
ELEC – electoral votes received by winning party (2016)
POP – population (millions) Iraq–39
GDP – gross domestic product (billion dollars) United Kingdom–2651
AREA – land area (1000 square miles) Iraq–169
COAST – coastline (statute miles)

PROM–Promisedland

61 – FEDERALLAND

The single state that makes up Federalland comprises a region that will be substantially autonomous, like the other lands of the new-USA, but which will also be the geographical location of the federal government. An alternative name might be Americaland. That new federal government is a fraction the size of its predecessor in the former District of Columbia, since its duties and powers are greatly reduced. It nonetheless will be an important contributor to the economy of Hawaii, which is roughly the size of Kuwait. Its population will rank it among the smallest countries (although it may be expected to grow with a modest influx of federal workers), as will its area. Its foreign policy will probably be assertive, but it will be reminded frequently and forcefully by the other former USA lands that it does not speak for them. Its domestic policies will undoubtedly be liberal, based on the record of both DC and Hawaii. Its presidential candidates will probably be indigenous, since the focus of that job will be on Hawaii. Candidates for the top *federal* job (perhaps called "Chief Magistrate", in the words of George Washington) may include Hillary Clinton, Joe Biden, and John Kerry, although the job may lack sufficient power to interest such high-profile people.

ST	PTY	ELEC	POP	GDP	AREA	COAST
HI	D	3	1.4	84	6	1052
FED	1	3	1.4	84	6	1052

ST – state postal code
PTY – winning party in 2016 election
ELEC – electoral votes received by winning party (2016)
POP – population (millions) Estonia – 1
GDP – gross domestic product (billion dollars) Cuba – 87
AREA – land area (1000 square miles) Kuwait – 7
COAST – coastline (statute miles)

FED–Federalland

Chapter 7
Reparations

Unlike the untying of the United States of America, reparations for slavery has long been both thinkable and speakable, as we shall see. This is not to say that it has enjoyed general support, however, for it has not, not even among African-Americans. It may be timely, on the other hand, to use reparations as a means of addressing the worsening racial divide in the country, even as the separation of regions is proposed as a means of addressing the geographical divide. When repeated efforts to bridge a divide have failed, it may be time to consider a different approach.

"Forty acres and a mule" was perhaps the earliest reparations promise/demand, and was briefly realized on a limited basis. In 1865, General Sherman issued Special Field Orders No.15, which granted the use of some number of acres (the mules were provided informally) to each of about 40,000 freed slave families on land in Georgia and South Carolina. This order was reversed by President Johnson shortly after President Lincoln was assassinated, and the land was returned to its previous owners. Two years later a bill was introduced in Congress to provide for land reparations to former slaves, but it was not passed. Subsequent legislative and other efforts for reparations have not been successful, but this has not been for lack of trying.

Rev. Dr. Jeremiah Wright was the keynote speaker at the 20th anniversary meeting, in 2007 in Philadelphia, of N'COBRA, the National Coalition of Blacks for Reparations in America. The reparations demands of the group have been estimated at $8 trillion, to be paid by the US government. The Republic of New Afrika was established in Detroit in 1968, but is now based in Washington, with a claimed membership of almost 10,000. Their demand is for an independent black nation to be made up of five Southern states, plus $400 billion, presumably also to be paid by the US government. The Afrikan World Reparations & Repatriation Truth Commission was established in 1998 in Ghana, and demands $777 trillion (roughly a decade's worth of total world production) to be paid by "former colonial countries" (presumably also including the US government). None of these demands appear to be close to realization, but the concept persists.

Some abolitionists pressed for reparations as well as freedom for slaves, but since the Civil War the cause has been pursued largely by African-Americans. Early in the 20th Century there was lobbying for federal pensions for former slaves, and a $68 million reparations lawsuit was filed in federal court. Representative John Conyers, a founder of the Black Congressional Caucus, in 1993 and subsequently has promoted a bill calling for a federal apology for slavery, and establishing a commission to investigate the effects on black Americans of racial and economic discrimination allegedly emanating from generations of slavery. The Conyers bill has not been passed by Congress, but it has been endorsed by numerous city councils, including those of Dallas and Fort Worth. Government bodies from city councils to state legislatures have also passed resolutions apologizing for slavery, or endorsing reparations, or both.

Reparations, by whatever name, has not been restricted to payments to black Americans as compensation for slavery and racial discrimination. Since 1953, Germany has paid about $100 billion to Israel and Holocaust survivors. Swiss banks and other financial institutions in the West have acknowledged their roles in the Holocaust and, in some cases, have made payments. Australia has paid reparations to aborigines, Canada to the Inuit, and Chile to Mapuche people. President Reagan signed the Civil Liberties Act of 1988 which provided about $20,000 to each of the 60,000 survivors (about half) of President Roosevelt's 1942 Executive Order 9066, which put Japanese-Americans in concentration camps. Finally, as noted above, while it is never called "reparations", the Indian Gaming Regulatory Act of 1988 has led to an industry with gross revenues of about $20 billion annually.

There are, of course, cogent arguments against reparations for slavery (some are muted when the payments are said to be for racism or racial discrimination), such as the following. Free people should not be compensated for slavery inflicted on others, even on their ancestors. Northern families who lost about 350,000 Union soldiers in the war to end slavery should not bear further burden due to the transgressions of a similar number of Southern slaveholders. Furthermore, the lines are not clearly drawn long after the crime has ended. Immediately prior to the Civil War there were several thousand black slaveowners, and in the previous century there were a number of white slaves. Persons from foreign countries who became American citizens during the 20th Century (Holocaust survivors, for example) should not be required to pay American blacks for a 19th Century crime. It may not be feasible to identify the descendants of slaves.

It may be feasible, however, to resolve this persistent and divisive issue by means of substantial reparations coupled with *voluntary* relocation by the recipients. Those "substantial reparations" are herein proposed to be the entirety of residential real estate in the former state of California. While less than the $8 trillion demanded by N'COBRA, the offer is a serious one currently worth several trillion dollars at least and including a large number of the most desirable homes in the world. There will be a number of issues to be resolved, it is true, but the alternative of failing to treat a wound that never heals has issues as well, and is eventually fatal.

The quid pro quo of separation for reparations is essential to the success of the plan. Each qualified beneficiary will have the option of receiving at no cost a California home, provided only that he/she and his/her family actually relocate to that home. See below for preliminary details of the plan.

Eligibility to receive reparations will be established by the Constitutional Convention set up for the primary purpose of untying the United States of America. Details and implementation will be by the American Slavery & Racism Reparations Trust (pronounced and denoted "ASSERT"), an agency of Promisedland, the former California. As implied by the name of the trust, strict proof that an ancestor was a slave will not be required. Proof will be required, however, presumably by DNA testing, that the applicant is a person of color, and that that color is black. A minimum quotient (say, 25%) of blackness (not skin color) will be required to receive a reparations home.

Each qualifying black person in the country will have the option, exercisable during the reparations transition period (say, 10 years), of accepting the offer and moving to Promisedland. Considerations will undoubtedly range from the practical (comparative job opportunities) to the personal (decisions by family and friends) to the intangible (degree of perceived oppression currently). Planning for the new country (and its counterparts) will necessarily require not only estimations of the proportion (perhaps 50%) of black Americans who will accept reparations, but also the demographic and other characteristics of those persons and families. ASSERT will acquire, on the day that Promisedland is established, full title to all residential property (including improvements) in the former state of California. It will operate under a controlled mandate established by the Constitutional Convention, but will gradually over the reparations transition period assume full independence. It will distribute acquired properties (see below) in accordance with transparent rules, subject only to approval by the citizens of Promisedland.

The only compulsion in the proposed reparations plan will be that all residential property in California be sold to ASSERT. This will be justified legally by the doctrine of eminent domain, with healing the wounds caused by slavery and racism put forth as the compelling public need justifying the compulsion. Compensation to the homeowner will be in cash, paid immediately to any bank or other lienholder, with remaining equity paid to the homeowner over the course of the reparations transition period, or upon vacating the premises. The price will be market value (a job for a truly independent commission) plus a modest margin (say, 10%) to recognize the homeowner's contribution to the public good. The homeowner will not be required to leave his or her home during the reparations transition period, but will pay rent to ASSERT at a rate to be determined. Whether the former homeowner will subsequently be required to move will depend on legislation to be enacted by the new Promisedland. Black Californians who currently own their homes may be in a particularly enviable position, if they qualify for reparations and are permitted by ASSERT to retain their homes, for they will have their mortgages paid off immediately and will subsequently receive cash equal to their equity in the home, plus a margin based on the "selling" price.

The distributing of California houses and condos and trailers will be determined by ASSERT, subject to diminishing (over time) authority in accordance with rules established by the Constitutional Convention. The allocation of homes as they become available (when people leave) may take account of such variables as degree of qualification for reparations, current living conditions, ability to pay the ongoing costs of the home, anticipated contribution to the success of Promisedland, and more. The use of a lottery may be considered, with every entrant a winner, although some more so than others. Gaining title to the home will require a continuous period (perhaps ten years) of occupancy and care of the home. The reparations beneficiary will be free to leave the home and Promisedland at any time (an essential outcome of the Constitutional Convention discussed in Chapter Six must be that anyone is free to emigrate from any of the new lands at any time for any reason), but may not be able to return to his or her former home since the new lands will be free to enact and enforce such immigration laws as they separately may see fit.

The source of all the cash alluded to above (perhaps $3 trillion, paid out over ten years, but considerably front-loaded) will presumably be the other seven new lands (the former California and perhaps Hawaii exempted). These lands will inherit, proportionately, the assets (public lands, public buildings, trust funds, taxes due, tanks and nukes, etc.) and liabilities (public debt, social insurance promises, etc.) of the former United States of America. This can be considered to be no bargain, since the excess of liabilities over assets probably exceeds $50 trillion. On the other hand, each new land will be free to revise or even repudiate its inherited debts and liabilities, an action that, however necessary, will not be without consequences. The remaining question is whether American voters, however defined, will be willing to accept the above reparations plan, or a reasonable facsimile thereof.

The first step to answering the question may well be to put the estimated $3 trillion price tag into perspective. While hardly inconsequential, it is a pale shadow (well under 10%) of the unfunded debt of Social Security and Medicare, currently scheduled to be dumped on future generations. It also bears promise of reducing or ending the ongoing transfer of money from whites (and others) to blacks – which may or may not have any basis in fact, but which is believed to be true by many of those who will be called upon to support the reparations plan. There will probably also be a considerable demographic shift in the country, if the untying of the states and the reparations plans are adopted, which arguably will be beneficial for all. African-Americans who accept the reparations offer will be those for whom the appeal of a free California home outweighs the net benefits of continuing to live in their white-dominated home state – and many if not most of this group will assess those net benefits to be zero, or less. African-Americans who decline the offer will presumably be those who not only see net benefits to staying where they are, but who assess those benefits as being greater than the value of a California home. Other Americans will reap the benefits of greatly reduced racial tensions and of retaining as neighbors those African-Americans who generally like being their neighbors, and of separating from those who do not. California is a nice place to visit (and ASSERT will surely want to maintain the tourism industry in good order), but you can't own a home there, unless you're a reparations beneficiary.

Chapter 8

Confederation

Any disparaging tone in these pages toward the federal government of the United States of America should not be imputed to the confederation government of the Untied States of America. It's true that the powers of the new federal (confederation) government will be less than those intended and established by the Founding Fathers in 1787, which in turn turned out to be a pale shadow of those that came to be usurped by the federal governments of the 20th and 21st Centuries, but the duly-limited powers of that new federal government nonetheless will be essential to the success of the new-USA. Those limited powers will include three functions, discussed below:

- Manage the transition from the old-USA to the new-USA;

- Oversee the operations of the American Slavery & Racism Reparations Trust (ASSERT) during the reparations transition period;

- Mediate disputes among the nine new lands making up the new-USA.

The Constitutional Convention, provided for in Article V of the US Constitution and leading to the untying of the United States of America will be faced with the challenge of being specific about plans for the Convention vision without at the same time slipping into a futile effort to micromanage an uncertain future. The Articles of Confederation (or another, original and better, name) must describe the new confederation government in some detail, clearly identifying both its responsibilities and its limits. One of those responsibilities will be the huge task of managing the transition from old-USA to new-USA. A major element of this change will be the dispersal of power from Washington, DC, to the capitals of nine new lands. Federal assets and liabilities, discussed above, will need to be distributed in accordance with goals and rules agreed upon at the Constitutional Convention. A timetable for the transition will be a desirable Convention goal, with a decade or less being a reasonable target, but there should be provision for amendment of the completion date if necessary. The important thing is that the transition period should be finite, and that the confederation government should be completely out of the transition business within a decade or so.

A second function of the confederation government will be to oversee the operations of the American Slavery & Racism Reparations Trust during the reparations transition period of perhaps ten years. The process by which ASSERT is established, and the rules under which it will operate, will be set forth in the Articles of Confederation. The Board of Directors of ASSERT will presumably be made up substantially if not exclusively of reparations beneficiaries who have exercised their option to live in the former California. The role of the confederation government will be limited to seeing that the reparations plan is operated in accordance with the Articles of Confederation, with particular emphasis on the collection and providing of money for the purpose.

An important ongoing function of the confederation government will be to mediate (not judge) disputes among the nine lands. This may be done administratively, where feasible, or by recourse to ad hoc commissions where not. Commission and other confederation costs will be borne by the disputants, which should encourage lands with issues to resolve them amicably without involving the federal government unless necessary.

The confederation government will be headquartered in the former Hawaii, even as its federal predecessor was headquartered in the District of Columbia, and may have offices in other US lands, with their permission. It may even have offices in foreign countries, subject to the clear understanding that it does not represent, and is not itself, a country, but rather a confederation of nine sovereign countries. It will have no taxing authority, other than as may be provided in the Articles of Confederation, and then only to enable it to carry out its limited duties. It will issue no currency, it will have no army.

The confederation government will be separate and distinct from Federalland, the former state of Hawaii, and from the government of that small new country. The District of Columbia will cease to have a federal function, and will be an administrative unit (perhaps called a state) of the large new country, Progressiveland.

Chapter 9

Prognosis

As this is being written (2018) a clear and probable political prognosis for the country is not evident. At least two alternative prognoses are required.

Consider first Prognosis A, under which Republicans narrowly retain control of both houses of Congress in the 2018 elections, and of the Administration, presumably but not necessarily under President Trump, in the 2020 election. Misreading the election results as a mandate, the Republican Congress passes, and the President signs, legislation that significantly reduces the federal role in healthcare, effectively closes the border to undocumented immigrants, and modestly rolls back recent progressive victories in some social areas. Meanwhile, the President makes appointments and the Senate confirms justices to the US Supreme Court, which transforms the Court into a reliably conservative body, pursues a fairly aggressive and nationalistic policy, and continues to roll back federal regulations. The right begins to feel that it has rescued the country from a corrupt socialism, while the left fears that the worst excesses of Trump's policies lie ahead.

Consider next Prognosis B, under which Democrats narrowly take control of both houses of Congress in 2018, and of the Administration in the 2020 election. Misreading the election results as a mandate, the Democrat Congress passes, and after 2020 the new President signs, legislation that establishes universal single-payer health insurance, that extends refugee status to immigrants seeking relief from economic or other oppression, and impeaches President Trump, but is unable to remove him from office until 2021. Thereafter the new President appoints and the Senate confirms justices to the US Supreme Court who will bring about a resumption of progressive updating of the Constitution; the President hires executive branch employees who will enforce a progressive interpretation of enacted legislation; and the President restores a foreign policy based on international norms. The left begins to feel that it has survived the existential challenge of the Trump years, and the right fears that the end of the American experiment in self-government is underway.

The confidence of either the right (Prognosis A) or left (Prognosis B) that their preferred course for the country will prevail will be short-lived, however, as the respective losers reject and resist trends that they see as existential threats to their cause. Under Prognosis A the resistance will take the form of rejection of conservative programs and policies by hold-over federal and other jurists, Senators, and bureaucrats, especially but not exclusively in so-called blue states. Under Prognosis B the resistance will similarly reject liberal programs and policies by federal and other holdovers, especially but not exclusively in so-called red states, as well as by civil disobedience to an even greater extent than their counterparts under Prognosis A. Most alarming, however, will be the increase in frequency and severity of violent demonstrations under either Prognosis. Further exacerbating the conflict under Prognosis A will be the power of the fourth estate (the media) in its new role as a fifth column (a group that works against the leaders of a country), and under Prognosis B will be the escalating use of guns (the vast majority of which are held by persons on the right) in demonstrations and elsewhere.

The national divide between the races (at least, the black/white divide) has been addressed in these pages, and a plausible if drastic solution put forth for consideration. The ideological divide in the country is less distinct, but can be reasonably if roughly described in terms of freedom/individualism versus collectivism/cooperation, or even simply in terms of more or less government. Republicans and Democrats imperfectly represent the two ideological camps, but it's an imperfect world, and our political system has been structured accordingly. The regions/lands are comprised of states that generally fall on one or the other side of the divide, even if only by a 51% standard. The groupings of the map are striking, even under the 2016 election, and illustrate clearly that the country is not united, and that the differences are regional to an important extent. It has been pointed out that there are significant ideological differences between regions that share the same voting pattern. Greenland and Unionland both generally vote Democratic, for example, but their primary interests are quite different (as is reflected in their names). The same is true at the state level, with regional connections sometimes trumping political party connections. Nevadans, even Nevada Democrats, very likely have more in common with the citizens of Arizona than they do with the citizens of Massachusetts. If the map on the cover could be heard, it would be crying out for the states to be untied from the current federal government, and to be united with their adjoining peers. Especially if the alternative is another civil war.

The United States of America is divided as it has not been for more than a century. To over-simplify, but to make the point, half the country wants more government, while half wants less. Half the country believes that they alone have compassion, and that their opponents are motivated primarily by their love of money. The other half believes that they alone appreciate freedom, and that their opponents are motivated by their lust for power. Political power oscillates between the halves, never staying for long on either side because of a relatively few swing voters who strive to maintain a precarious balance. An increasing proportion of the electorate is on or near one seat or the other of the national seesaw, and the view of the opposing seat is increasingly one of fear and loathing. Each side believes fervently that the world (or the country, at least) will be a better place when they prevail, but this sanguine emotion is overcome by terror at the perceived sanguinary nature of the opponent. Thus the seesaw continues to move back and forth, and forth and back, with each cycle lodging more and more people filled with more and more fear and loathing at either end of the plank. This is the very definition of the build-up to a civil war.

The hatred of Trump by those on the left is best understood by realizing the threat he poses to their successful expansion of government over the past century. Government at all levels controlled less than one-tenth of the economy 100 years ago, but today controls about two-thirds. The Progressive Era had an early peak in the teens of the 20th Century with the 1913 establishment of the Federal Reserve Board (which has presided over the drop in value of the dollar to less than a nickel), the 1913 amendment of the Constitution to permit income taxation (thereby providing the means for government expansion), and passage starting in 1914 with state control of the first social insurance program (workers' compensation insurance). After a pause during the Coolidge years, the Progressive Era resumed and expanded during Roosevelt's New Deal and for decades thereafter, including even the Eisenhower years (when Congress was firmly controlled by Democrats). After a second pause during the Reagan years, progressive causes continued to expand up to the Obama years, when they expanded at a rate reminiscent of the New Deal. Trump's victory in 2016, after a campaign targeting progressive causes, was a body blow to the left. Worse still, Republicans gained narrow control of both houses of Congress, and Trump's early Presidency was marked by strict adherence to his campaign promises. Democrats united as never before to resist the Trump Presidency, and to deny his policies and programs "by any means necessary". Their resistance will not subside over the years ahead since Trump represents less a pause than a reversal. As viewed from outside the country, the USA will be preoccupied and weakened by internal political and civil fighting and escalating domestic violence. We won't need to be actually in CWII to be vulnerable.

The weakened state of the United States will be noticed by our competitors and adversaries around the world, and acted upon by some of them. We will surely feel trade pressures from the European Union and China, and perhaps beyond. Russia and/or China may be emboldened to launch military challenges against the US and, although self-preservation may cause either or both of them to stop short of a nuclear attack, such restraint may not be shown by North Korea and/or Iran. Part of the equation may be that a unified defense of the formerly united states cannot be assured, in part because some on the left hate not only Donald Trump, but also the country he leads (or led).

The best chance for defense of the continent we share may be brought about by the common interests of the nine lands made up of the untied states of the former USA, along with help from our neighbors to the north and south.

Chapter 10

Answers to Some Likely Questions

1. **Are you serious?** As you wish. If not, the book is a parlor game, a diversion for those who enjoy flights of fancy involving politics and statistics. But the ideological and racial divides in the USA are serious, especially since they appear to be worsening, with or without another civil war in our future. It is clear that solutions to our divisions will not happen with a business-as-usual approach. The unthinkable must become thinkable, and discussible, if we are to improve the future that is unfolding before us and our children.

2. **Why reparations?** It's not just that the ideological and racial divides in the country are serious, which they surely are. Although inconclusive concerning the racial divide, the evidence is strong that both splits are widening, and surely the conversation across the growing chasms is becoming less civil by the day. Every landlord knows that two renters who are intolerable to each other as roommates are better off in different rooms. You very likely know people, perhaps quite a few, with whom you can be civil or even cordial across the fence dividing your houses, but not if you must share a home. Some portion of African-Americans clearly would prefer to live in a land where they are in the majority, rather than where they

must accommodate to white or brown laws, customs, and attitudes. Others would not, or don't care. The option of relocating to Promisedland, now a black-run independent country, will permit those in the former group to get out from under the oppression they currently feel, or merely to join others with whom they share common interests. Reparations, in the form of all California residential real estate, will make this option feasible. Many Americans, black and white, believe that substantial reparations are due to African-Americans because of historical slavery or ongoing racial discrimination or both. Many others disagree, but will accept the proposed reparations plan as providing a solution to an otherwise intractable problem. Some may even consider the separation of California to be a good thing.

3. **Is your plan Constitutional?** Maybe, maybe not. The Constitution does provide, in Article V, for amendments to be initiated by the states, and does not therein limit the content or scope of such amendments. It goes on to state that the Constitution shall be the "supreme Law of the Land", superseding any contradictory State law, but that provision could be considered and even accommodated during the Constitutional Convention that is proposed to bring about the untying of the united states. Indeed, that untying might consist of little more than the resuscitation and strengthening of the moribund Tenth Amendment, which states that "the powers not delegated to the United States by the Constitution, nor prohibited by it to the States, are reserved to the States respectively, or to the people".

4. **Does this plan take us back to segregation?** Hardly. Voluntary relocation to a free home in California bears little resemblance to the racial segregation that was mandated or tolerated during much of the 19th and 20th Centuries. Furthermore, those who wish not to relocate will be under no obligation to do so. The cost of the reparations plan, consisting substantially of paying current Californians for the homes they are turning over to ASSERT, will be the same irrespective of the numbers that

accept or decline the reparations offer. Acceptance or rejection by beneficiaries of the offer will be strictly voluntary.

5. **Will the new lands be free to control their borders?** There are two answers to this question. Yes, with regard to immigration. Each land will be free to build literal or figurative fences, or not, as they wish, as befits the sovereign countries that they will become. No, with regard to emigration. It is expected that the Constitutional Convention will result in few restrictions on the new lands, but that one of those restrictions will be the requirement that all persons, citizens or not, will be free to emigrate at any time (subject perhaps to certain exceptions, such as being indicted for or convicted of a major crime). This simple rule, if imposed and enforced by the civilized world on murderous regimes, would have saved many millions of lives during the 20th Century.

6. **Suppose one of the new lands does terrible things to its people, or to visitors?** One man's terrible thing may be a thing of beauty in the eye of a different beholder, but it must be acknowledged that some things fail to meet even the minimum standards of polite society. Intraland acceptance of free emigration (see #5 above), however, will go a long way toward limiting transgressions without otherwise violating national sovereignty. Most of the many people killed by their governments during the 20th Century lived in lands with borders that were tightly controlled in an outbound direction.

7. **What demographic changes are expected as a result of the untying?** Some portion (say, 50%) of African-Americans may be expected to move to what was previously California, whereas another portion (say, 50%) of Californians may be expected to emigrate. The California population won't change much if those portions are similar, since the current population of California is only about 15% more than that of black America (there is some overlap, in that California is currently about 6% African-American). The outflow and inflow of other lands may

vary, but there seems to be no reason to expect major population shifts, except probably from the District of Columbia into California and perhaps into Hawaii. Some persons in the ideological minority in the new lands may relocate to another land more of their liking, but streets clogged with refugees escaping Seattle or Miami seems an unlikely scenario.

8. **Who gets the nukes?** Military assets of the United States of America, including nuclear weapons, will be distributed among the new lands in proportion to population. The former state of Hawaii may get an extra allocation, both to recognize its geographic isolation and to provide it with the means to protect the Confederation government.

9. **Who gets the national debt?** The national debt is not just the $20+ trillion acknowledged debt, but also includes the much larger social insurance debt, plus the unfunded federal retiree debt, plus the debt to be incurred for bailing out Fanny Mae and Freddie Mac and other financial institutions, not to mention all the other federal government protectorates. This huge debt, equal to five or more years of GDP, will be distributed among the lands proportional to the size of the land's economy. Each land will deal with its inherited debt in its own way, balancing the needs of its citizens (retirees, young workers, etc) against the demands of arithmetic (two loaves and five fish will not suffice to feed the multitudes). This may involve partial repudiation of the government debt, of course, but this will be true whether the states remain tied or become untied.

10. **Why are there so many numbers in the book?** Partly because the author is an actuary, but largely to establish that the proposed lands are viable by any measure, and should be well able to establish themselves among the countries of the world.

11. **Where will the non-black Californians go?** Some will no doubt take their money (consisting of their home equity plus 10% of the established value of the home) and move to another

land, or beyond. Others will decide to stay, as renters in the houses they formerly owned, or in other California homes. Most current Californians already are renters, who themselves may decide to leave or stay. None will be required to leave, either their homes or California, at least not during the reparations transition period. After that period, all inhabitants of the former California will be subject to the laws of Promisedland, which conceivably (if not likely) could include expulsions, though not involuntary detentions (see #5 above).

12. **Suppose some states don't want to untie?** The Constitution provides for its own amendment when three-fourths of the states agree to the proposed change. Many if not most of the amendments that have passed did so over substantial opposition, yet all have been accepted by all of the states, however grudgingly. At least one of the amendments (Amendment XIII, banning slavery) arguably had as much or more impact on the lives of many Americans than will the proposed untying of the states. The period of debate may be lengthy, from proposal to ratification, but it is unlikely to set a new record in that regard (Amendment XXVII was proposed in 1789 and ratified in 1992).

13. **What timing is foreseen for this proposal to be realized?** It's a fool's errand to predict the length of time it will take for the country to think the unthinkable, consider the considerable, and convene the Convention. While it is certain that the USA as currently structured will not last forever, it remains to be seen whether its change to a different structure will be controlled by its citizens, as is proposed herein, or whether it will be occasioned by events beyond their control. Most major changes simmer for a long while, and then happen with surprising speed following a triggering event. Consider Fort Sumter in this regard, or even Pearl Harbor. An external triggering event, such as a truly massive terrorist attack, is more likely to bring the country together, if only temporarily, than to burst it asunder. An internal triggering event, on the other

hand, could be just the catalyst needed to choose untying over another War Between the States. Such an event could be the financial strains or collapse that will be inevitable as the country's social insurance debts come due. This conceivably could lead to a Constitutional Convention in, say, 2035, and to nine new lands on the world scene as early as 2040.

14. **What about reparations for disadvantaged groups other than African Americans?** As our history shows, no group has as strong a claim for redress than the former slaves and, arguably, their descendants. Native Americans may dispute that assertion but, as put forth above, Indian Gaming Laws can certainly be viewed as reparations, whatever the legal niceties. Hispanics in America now outnumber African-Americans but, with few exceptions, they and their ancestors came voluntarily to this country. They and many other groups (disabled persons, Muslims, gays, women, short people, etc.) are surely entitled to protection under civil rights legislation, but few would argue that they should receive reparations.

15. **The USA will give up most of its strength if it disintegrates, will it not?** It will not. It (or rather, they) will probably be stronger by most measures, at least relative to where the USA is headed. Consider the financial debacle that will surely unfold during the collapse of our social insurance systems. With over $100 trillion of debt coming due, and no means of retiring it short of debasing the currency or simply refusing to pay, the term "full faith and credit of the US Government" is bound to become a bad joke, or worse. The nine new lands will not be able entirely to escape the fallout from the fiscal irresponsibility (indeed, fiscal child abuse) of the 20th Century and beyond, but they will be able to seek their own individual paths to restructuring their inherited debt and salvaging their economies. Some will do better than others, no doubt, but all will have the opportunity to chart their course in accordance with the wishes of a majority of their citizens, rather than to be hobbled like rival

conjoined siblings, unable to compete or cooperate effectively in the world economy.

16. **Will not most other countries be appalled at the breakup of the United States?** They will not. In fact, many will rejoice. The USA, for all its attraction as a land of (relative) freedom, is widely perceived as dominant and intrusive, seeking to impose its will on other sovereign nations. Furthermore, there is ample precedent for worldwide or wide acceptance of breakaway provinces, such as "the Ukraine" (which is smaller than Dixieland in both area and population, and smaller than all but one of the new lands in GDP) following the breakup of the Soviet Union. In this century, many countries have recognized Kosovo, and a few have recognized the contested provinces of Georgia.

17. **Why now, when all candidates for office promise hope and change and a bright, new tomorrow?** Please.

18. **Why are the Second Civil War scenarios so sketchy?** The purpose of this book is to encourage the reader to think the unthinkable, to recognize that we may be headed toward another civil war at some time in our national future, and to consider ways to avert that fatal calamity. It's possible to discern and project trends, such as a growing divide over the appropriate role of the federal government. It's far more difficult to foresee and foretell the triggering event that will result in that thinkable if not predictable Second Civil War. The scenarios in Chapters 5 and 9 sketch ways in which divisive national problems (response to terrorism, post-election crises) could develop so as to lead to the triggering event in question. The author will be gratified if readers improve upon these scenarios, or develop new ones based on these or other divisive national problems.

19. **Will not the new lands wage war upon one another?** Perhaps. But it is not inevitable that neighboring countries will go to war. The USA has had profound differences with its neighbors on both the north and south, but has had no warlike conflict

with either for more than a century. It will be important that the Constitutional Convention carefully consider potential conflicts between the new lands, and provide the new Confederation government with the tools to mediate (not arbitrate) conflicts as they arise. The majority citizen in each of the new lands will be relieved to be the permanent captain of his or her own destiny, rather than vacillating between euphoria and despair every multiple of four years. The minority citizen will either be content in his role of tempering the excesses of the majority, or will exercise his inalienable right to emigrate. In any event, the likelihood of a new War Between the (new) States is much less than that of Civil War II.

20. **Is not your depiction of the national divide, as being between those who want more versus less government, overly simplistic?** No, it's just simple enough. It's not entirely true that the left, the progressives, the Democrats want a stronger federal government in all cases (most would bar the government at the door to your bedroom), even though they do generally want power as a means of helping oppressed persons overcome their oppression at the hands of the (private) establishment. It's not entirely true that the right, the conservatives, the Republicans want a weaker federal government in all cases (most want that government to take down a foreign government that foments terrorism directed at the US), even though they do want limits on the federal government as a means of preserving individual freedoms (and local government). It's not entirely nor solely true that the acknowledged and widening and deepening national divide is between two camps that simply want more versus less federal government, but it's close enough for working purposes.

APPENDIX A

Countries of the World

Appendix A contains information about the countries of the world, including the United States of America and, as well, the nine new lands that together make up the Untied States of America. It is presented in four sections, as follows:

- Appendix A1 – alphabetical order

- Appendix A2 – population sort

- Appendix A3 – area sort

- Appendix A4 – GDP sort

The top part of each section contains data about the nine lands and about the Untied States of America, including for each the following:

- Number of states (including the District of Columbia)

- Electoral votes per state (2012 and 2016 elections)

- Population (in millions)

- Land area (in thousands of square miles)

- Gross domestic product (in billions of dollars)

The bottom part of Appendix A1 runs to several pages, since it lists every country in the world (including the USA and the nine new lands) with GDP greater than $6 billion. The list has 144 entries, consisting of 135 existing countries plus the 9 new lands. It excludes 62 countries that don't make the GDP cutoff, or for other reasons.

State data is from the 2018 edition of the Statistical Abstract of the United States as follows (parenthetical references are to Tables in the book): electoral votes (442), population (14), area (394), and gross domestic product (694). Country data is from that same book (Table 1353), or from underlying source data provided by The World Bank.

Appendix A2 contains A1 data sorted by population, and limited to the 100 largest countries by that measure (which includes eight of the nine new lands), including the United States of America (which has the same population as the Untied States of America). While none of the new lands would be among the 20 largest countries (the USA is third largest), six of them would be among the 50 largest countries in terms of population.

Appendix A3 contains A1 data sorted by area, again limited to the 100 largest countries, including the USA. Area measurements include land only within the boundaries of the respective countries, but the world total excludes Antarctica, at about 5.4 million square miles. The list again includes eight of the nine new lands, including one in the top 10 and two in the 20 largest countries in terms of geography.

Appendix A4 contains A1 data sorted by gross national product, again limited to the 100 largest countries, including the USA. The list now includes all nine new lands, including four in the top 10 and eight in the 25 largest countries in terms of economic output.

Appendix A shows clearly that each of the nine proposed new lands is viable among the countries of the world in terms of population and area and, perhaps most important, gross national product. Seven of the lands would rank among the powerhouse economies of the world, with economies larger than $1 trillion annually, with six of the seven being larger, by this measure, than either of our neighbors to the north and south.

LANDS:	STATES	ELEC	POP	AREA	GDP
APPALACHIA	5	53	31	181	1567
DIXIE	7	97	62	327	2987
FEDERAL	1	4	1	6	84
GREEN	2	19	11	162	697
HEART	10	92	55	853	3004
PROGRESSIVE	12	112	64	174	4365
PROMISED	1	55	39	156	2603
ROCKY	9	50	25	1426	1226
UNION	4	56	34	246	1924
TOTAL	51	538	322	3531	18457

COUNTRIES:			POP	AREA	GDP
AFGHANISTAN			34	252	19
ALBANIA			3	11	12
ALGERIA			41	920	159
ANGOLA			29	481	95
* **APPALACHIALAND**			**31**	**181**	**1567**
ARGENTINA			44	1057	555
ARMENIA			3	11	11
AUSTRALIA			23	2966	1208
AUSTRIA			9	32	391
AZERBAIJAN			10	32	38
BANGLADESH			158	50	221
BELARUS			10	78	48
BELGIUM			11	12	468
BOLIVIA			11	418	34
BOSNIA AND HERZEGOVINA			4	20	17
BOTSWANA			2	219	16
BRAZIL			207	3227	1794
BULGARIA			7	42	53
BURKINA FASO			20	106	11
BURMA			55	252	63
CAMBODIA			16	68	20
CAMEROON			25	183	32
CANADA			36	3511	1536
CHAD			12	486	9
CHILE			18	287	250
CHINA			1379	3601	11191
COLOMBIA			48	401	280
CONGO			83	875	35

APPENDIX A1 - COUNTRIES OF THE WORLD - ALPHABETICAL SORT

COUNTRIES:	POP	AREA	GDP
CONGO REPUBLIC	5	132	8
COSTA RICA	5	20	57
COTE D'IVOIRE	24	123	36
CROATIA	4	22	51
CUBA	11	42	87
CZECH REPUBLIC	11	30	195
DENMARK	6	16	307
* **DIXIELAND**	**62**	**327**	**2987**
DOMINICAN REPUBLIC	11	19	72
ECUADOR	16	107	99
EGYPT	97	384	333
EL SALVADOR	6	8	24
ESTONIA	1	16	23
ETHIOPIA	105	386	73
* **FEDERALLAND**	**1**	**6**	**84**
FINLAND	6	117	239
FRANCE	67	247	2465
GABON	2	99	14
GEORGIA	5	27	14
GERMANY	81	135	3478
GHANA	27	88	43
GREECE	11	50	193
* **GREENLAND**	**11**	**162**	**697**
GUATEMALA	15	41	69
* **HEARTLAND**	**55**	**853**	**3004**
HONDURAS	9	43	22
HUNGARY	10	35	126
INDIA	1282	1148	2274
INDONESIA	261	699	932
IRAN	82	591	419
IRAQ	39	169	171
IRELAND	5	27	305
ISRAEL	8	8	318
ITALY	62	114	1859
JAMAICA	3	4	14
JAPAN	126	140	4949
JORDAN	10	34	39
KAZAKHSTAN	19	1042	137
KENYA	48	220	71
NORTH KOREA	25	46	16
SOUTH KOREA	51	37	1415
KUWAIT	3	7	111

COUNTRIES:	POP	AREA	GDP
KYRGYZSTAN	6	74	7
LAOS	7	89	16
LATVIA	2	24	28
LEBANON	6	4	50
LIBYA	7	679	32
LITHUANIA	3	24	43
MACEDONIA	2	10	11
MADAGASCAR	25	225	10
MALAWI	19	36	5
MALAYSIA	31	127	297
MALI	18	471	14
MAURITIUS	1	1	12
MEXICO	125	751	1077
MONGOLIA	3	600	11
MOROCCO	34	172	104
MOZAMBIQUE	27	304	11
NAMIBIA	2	318	11
NEPAL	29	55	21
NETHERLANDS	17	13	777
NEW ZEALAND	5	102	189
NICARAGUA	6	46	13
NIGER	19	489	8
NIGERIA	191	351	405
NORWAY	5	117	371
OMAN	3	119	67
PAKISTAN	205	298	279
PANAMA	4	29	58
PAPUA NEW GUINEA	7	175	20
PARAGUAY	7	153	27
PERU	31	494	192
PHILIPPINES	104	115	305
POLAND	38	117	471
PORTUGAL	11	35	205
* **PROGRESSIVELAND**	**64**	**174**	**4365**
* **PROMISEDLAND**	**39**	**156**	**2603**
ROMANIA	22	89	188
* **ROCKYLAND**	**25**	**1426**	**1226**
RUSSIA	142	6323	1285
RWANDA	12	10	8
SAUDI ARABIA	29	830	645
SENEGAL	15	74	15
SERBIA	7	30	38

COUNTRIES:	POP	AREA	GDP
SINGAPORE	6	0	310
SLOVAKIA	5	19	90
SLOVENIA	2	8	45
SOUTH AFRICA	55	469	296
SOUTH SUDAN	13	249	3
SPAIN	49	193	1237
SRI LANKA	22	25	82
SUDAN	37	719	96
SWEDEN	10	158	514
SWITZERLAND	8	15	669
SYRIA	18	71	74
TAIWAN	24	12	531
TAJIKISTAN	8	55	7
TANZANIA	54	342	47
THAILAND	68	197	412
TRINIDAD AND TOBAGO	1	2	22
TUNISIA	11	60	42
TURKEY	81	297	864
TURKMENISTAN	5	181	36
UGANDA	40	76	24
UKRAINE	44	224	93
* **UNIONLAND**	**34**	**246**	**1924**
UNITED ARAB EMIRATES	6	32	357
UNITED KINGDOM	65	93	2651
* **UNITED STATES**	**322**	**3531**	**18457**
URUGUAY	3	68	53
UZBEKISTAN	30	164	67
VENEZUELA	31	341	371
VIETNAM	96	120	205
YEMEN	28	204	18
ZAMBIA	16	287	21
ZIMBABWE	14	149	17
SUBTOTAL	7256	48405	74661
ALL OTHER	149	2450	6022
WORLD	7405	50855	80683

LANDS:	STATES	ELEC	POP	AREA	GDP
PROGRESSIVE	12	112	64	174	4365
DIXIE	7	97	62	327	2987
HEART	10	92	55	853	3004
PROMISED	1	55	39	156	2603
UNION	4	56	34	246	1924
APPALACHIA	5	53	31	181	1567
ROCKY	9	50	25	1426	1226
GREEN	2	19	11	162	697
FEDERAL	1	4	1	6	84
TOTAL	51	538	322	3531	18457

COUNTRIES:	POP	AREA	GDP
CHINA	1379	3601	11191
INDIA	1282	1148	2274
* **UNITED STATES**	**322**	**3531**	**18457**
INDONESIA	261	699	932
BRAZIL	207	3227	1794
PAKISTAN	205	298	279
NIGERIA	191	351	405
BANGLADESH	158	50	221
RUSSIA	142	6323	1285
JAPAN	126	140	4949
MEXICO	125	751	1077
ETHIOPIA	105	386	73
PHILIPPINES	104	115	305
EGYPT	97	384	333
VIETNAM	96	120	205
CONGO	83	875	35
IRAN	82	591	419
GERMANY	81	135	3478
TURKEY	81	297	864
THAILAND	68	197	412
FRANCE	67	247	2465
UNITED KINGDOM	65	93	2651
* **PROGRESSIVELAND**	**64**	**174**	**4365**
* **DIXIELAND**	**62**	**327**	**2987**
ITALY	62	114	1859
BURMA	55	252	63
* **HEARTLAND**	**55**	**853**	**3004**
SOUTH AFRICA	55	469	296

COUNTRIES:	POP	AREA	GDP
TANZANIA	54	342	47
SOUTH KOREA	51	37	1415
SPAIN	49	193	1237
COLOMBIA	48	401	280
KENYA	48	220	71
ARGENTINA	44	1057	555
UKRAINE	44	224	93
ALGERIA	41	920	159
UGANDA	40	76	24
IRAQ	39	169	171
* **PROMISEDLAND**	**39**	**156**	**2603**
POLAND	38	117	471
SUDAN	37	719	96
CANADA	36	3511	1536
AFGHANISTAN	34	252	19
MOROCCO	34	172	104
* **UNIONLAND**	**34**	**246**	**1924**
* **APPALACHIALAND**	**31**	**181**	**1567**
MALAYSIA	31	127	297
PERU	31	494	192
VENEZUELA	31	341	371
UZBEKISTAN	30	164	67
ANGOLA	29	481	95
NEPAL	29	55	21
SAUDI ARABIA	29	830	645
YEMEN	28	204	18
GHANA	27	88	43
MOZAMBIQUE	27	304	11
CAMEROON	25	183	32
NORTH KOREA	25	46	16
MADAGASCAR	25	225	10
* **ROCKYLAND**	**25**	**1426**	**1226**
COTE D'IVOIRE	24	123	36
TAIWAN	24	12	531
AUSTRALIA	23	2966	1208
ROMANIA	22	89	188
SRI LANKA	22	25	82
BURKINA FASO	20	106	11
KAZAKHSTAN	19	1042	137
MALAWI	19	36	5
NIGER	19	489	8
CHILE	18	287	250

APPENDIX A2 - COUNTRIES OF THE WORLD - POPULATION SORT

COUNTRIES:	POP	AREA	GDP
MALI	18	471	14
SYRIA	18	71	74
NETHERLANDS	17	13	777
CAMBODIA	16	68	20
ECUADOR	16	107	99
ZAMBIA	16	287	21
GUATEMALA	15	41	69
SENEGAL	15	74	15
ZIMBABWE	14	149	17
SOUTH SUDAN	13	249	3
CHAD	12	486	9
RWANDA	12	10	8
BELGIUM	11	12	468
BOLIVIA	11	418	34
CUBA	11	42	87
CZECH REPUBLIC	11	30	195
DOMINICAN REPUBLIC	11	19	72
GREECE	11	50	193
* **GREENLAND**	**11**	**162**	**697**
PORTUGAL	11	35	205
TUNISIA	11	60	42
AZERBAIJAN	10	32	38
BELARUS	10	78	48
HUNGARY	10	35	126
JORDAN	10	34	39
SWEDEN	10	158	514
AUSTRIA	9	32	391
HONDURAS	9	43	22
ISRAEL	8	8	318
SWITZERLAND	8	15	669
SUBTOTAL	7067	44648	71462
ALL OTHER	338	6207	9221
WORLD	7405	50855	80683

71

LANDS:	STATES	ELEC	POP	AREA	GDP
ROCKY	9	50	25	1426	1226
HEART	10	92	55	853	3004
DIXIE	7	97	62	327	2987
UNION	4	56	34	246	1924
APPALACHIA	5	53	31	181	1567
PROGRESSIVE	12	112	64	174	4365
GREEN	2	19	11	162	697
PROMISED	1	55	39	156	2603
FEDERAL	1	4	1	6	84
TOTAL	51	538	322	3531	18457

COUNTRIES:	POP	AREA	GDP
RUSSIA	142	6323	1285
CHINA	1379	3601	11191
* **UNITED STATES**	**322**	**3531**	**18457**
CANADA	36	3511	1536
BRAZIL	207	3227	1794
AUSTRALIA	23	2966	1208
* **ROCKYLAND**	**25**	**1426**	**1226**
INDIA	1282	1148	2274
ARGENTINA	44	1057	555
KAZAKHSTAN	19	1042	137
ALGERIA	41	920	159
CONGO	83	875	35
* **HEARTLAND**	**55**	**853**	**3004**
SAUDI ARABIA	29	830	645
MEXICO	125	751	1077
SUDAN	37	719	96
INDONESIA	261	699	932
LIBYA	7	679	32
MONGOLIA	3	600	11
IRAN	82	591	419
PERU	31	494	192
NIGER	19	489	8
CHAD	12	486	9
ANGOLA	29	481	95
MALI	18	471	14
SOUTH AFRICA	55	469	296
BOLIVIA	11	418	34
COLOMBIA	48	401	280

COUNTRIES:	POP	AREA	GDP
ETHIOPIA	105	386	73
EGYPT	97	384	333
NIGERIA	191	351	405
TANZANIA	54	342	47
VENEZUELA	31	341	371
* **DIXIELAND**	**62**	**327**	**2987**
NAMIBIA	2	318	11
MOZAMBIQUE	27	304	11
PAKISTAN	205	298	279
TURKEY	81	297	864
CHILE	18	287	250
ZAMBIA	16	287	21
AFGHANISTAN	34	252	19
BURMA	55	252	63
SOUTH SUDAN	13	249	3
FRANCE	67	247	2465
* **UNIONLAND**	**34**	**246**	**1924**
MADAGASCAR	25	225	10
UKRAINE	44	224	93
KENYA	48	220	71
BOTSWANA	2	219	16
YEMEN	28	204	18
THAILAND	68	197	412
SPAIN	49	193	1237
CAMEROON	25	183	32
* **APPALACHIALAND**	**31**	**181**	**1567**
TURKMENISTAN	5	181	36
PAPUA NEW GUINEA	7	175	20
* **PROGRESSIVELAND**	**64**	**174**	**4365**
MOROCCO	34	172	104
IRAQ	39	169	171
UZBEKISTAN	30	164	67
* **GREENLAND**	**11**	**162**	**697**
SWEDEN	10	158	514
* **PROMISEDLAND**	**39**	**156**	**2603**
PARAGUAY	7	153	27
ZIMBABWE	14	149	17
JAPAN	126	140	4949
GERMANY	81	135	3478
CONGO REPUBLIC	5	132	8
MALAYSIA	31	127	297
COTE D'IVOIRE	24	123	36

APPENDIX A3 - COUNTRIES OF THE WORLD - AREA SORT

COUNTRIES:	POP	AREA	GDP
VIETNAM	96	120	205
OMAN	3	119	67
FINLAND	6	117	239
NORWAY	5	117	371
POLAND	38	117	471
PHILIPPINES	104	115	305
ITALY	62	114	1859
ECUADOR	16	107	99
BURKINA FASO	20	106	11
NEW ZEALAND	5	102	189
GABON	2	99	14
UNITED KINGDOM	65	93	2651
LAOS	7	89	16
ROMANIA	22	89	188
GHANA	27	88	43
BELARUS	10	78	48
UGANDA	40	76	24
KYRGYZSTAN	6	74	7
SENEGAL	15	74	15
SYRIA	18	71	74
CAMBODIA	16	68	20
URUGUAY	3	68	53
TUNISIA	11	60	42
NEPAL	29	55	21
TAJIKISTAN	8	55	7
BANGLADESH	158	50	221
GREECE	11	50	193
NORTH KOREA	25	46	16
NICARAGUA	6	46	13
HONDURAS	9	43	22
SUBTOTAL	6886	47523	67103
ALL OTHER	519	3332	13580
WORLD	7405	50855	80683

APPENDIX A4 - COUNTRIES OF THE WORLD - ECONOMY SORT

LANDS:	STATES	ELEC	POP	AREA	GDP
PROGRESSIVE	12	112	64	174	4365
HEART	10	92	55	853	3004
DIXIE	7	97	62	327	2987
PROMISED	1	55	39	156	2603
UNION	4	56	34	246	1924
APPALACHIA	5	53	31	181	1567
ROCKY	9	50	25	1426	1226
GREEN	2	19	11	162	697
FEDERAL	1	4	1	6	84
TOTAL	51	538	322	3531	18457

COUNTRIES:		POP	AREA	GDP
*	**UNITED STATES**	**322**	**3531**	**18457**
	CHINA	1379	3601	11191
	JAPAN	126	140	4949
*	**PROGRESSIVELAND**	**64**	**174**	**4365**
	GERMANY	81	135	3478
*	**HEARTLAND**	**55**	**853**	**3004**
*	**DIXIELAND**	**62**	**354**	**2987**
	UNITED KINGDOM	65	93	2651
*	**PROMISEDLAND**	**39**	**156**	**2603**
	FRANCE	67	247	2465
	INDIA	1282	1148	2274
*	**UNIONLAND**	**34**	**246**	**1924**
	ITALY	62	114	1859
	BRAZIL	207	3227	1794
*	**APPALACHIALAND**	**31**	**181**	**1567**
	CANADA	36	3511	1536
	SOUTH KOREA	51	37	1415
	RUSSIA	142	6323	1285
	SPAIN	49	193	1237
*	**ROCKYLAND**	**25**	**1426**	**1226**
	AUSTRALIA	23	2966	1208
	MEXICO	125	751	1077
	INDONESIA	261	699	932
	TURKEY	81	297	864
	NETHERLANDS	17	13	777
*	**GREENLAND**	**11**	**162**	**697**
	SWITZERLAND	8	15	669
	SAUDI ARABIA	29	830	645

APPENDIX A4 - COUNTRIES OF THE WORLD - ECONOMY SORT

COUNTRIES:	POP	AREA	GDP
ARGENTINA	44	1057	555
TAIWAN	24	12	531
SWEDEN	10	158	514
POLAND	38	117	471
BELGIUM	11	12	468
IRAN	82	591	419
THAILAND	68	197	412
NIGERIA	191	351	405
AUSTRIA	9	32	391
NORWAY	5	117	371
VENEZUELA	31	341	371
UNITED ARAB EMIRATES	6	32	357
EGYPT	97	384	333
ISRAEL	8	8	318
SINGAPORE	6	0	310
DENMARK	6	16	307
IRELAND	5	27	305
PHILIPPINES	104	115	305
MALAYSIA	31	127	297
SOUTH AFRICA	55	469	296
COLOMBIA	48	401	280
PAKISTAN	205	298	279
CHILE	18	287	250
FINLAND	6	117	239
BANGLADESH	158	50	221
PORTUGAL	11	35	205
VIETNAM	96	120	205
CZECH REPUBLIC	11	30	195
GREECE	11	50	193
PERU	31	494	192
NEW ZEALAND	5	102	189
ROMANIA	22	89	188
IRAQ	39	169	171
ALGERIA	41	920	159
KAZAKHSTAN	19	1042	137
HUNGARY	10	35	126
KUWAIT	3	7	111
MOROCCO	34	172	104
ECUADOR	16	107	99
SUDAN	37	719	96
ANGOLA	29	481	95
UKRAINE	44	224	93

COUNTRIES:	POP	AREA	GDP
SLOVAKIA	5	19	90
CUBA	11	42	87
* **FEDERALLAND**	**1**	**6**	**84**
SRI LANKA	22	25	82
SYRIA	18	71	74
ETHIOPIA	105	386	73
DOMINICAN REPUBLIC	11	19	72
KENYA	48	220	71
GUATEMALA	15	41	69
OMAN	3	119	67
UZBEKISTAN	30	164	67
BURMA	55	252	63
PANAMA	4	29	58
COSTA RICA	5	20	57
BULGARIA	7	42	53
URUGUAY	3	68	53
CROATIA	4	22	51
LEBANON	6	4	50
BELARUS	10	78	48
TANZANIA	54	342	47
SLOVENIA	2	8	45
GHANA	27	88	43
LITHUANIA	3	24	43
TUNISIA	11	60	42
JORDAN	10	34	39
AZERBAIJAN	10	32	38
SERBIA	7	30	38
COTE D'IVOIRE	24	123	36
TURKMENISTAN	5	181	36
CONGO	83	875	35
SUBTOTAL	6736	41428	73953
ALL OTHER	669	9427	6730
WORLD	7405	50855	80683

APPENDIX B

State and Land Statistics

Appendix B contains information about the 50 states (plus DC), and as well about the nine new lands that together make up the Untied States of America. It is presented in five sections, as follows:

- Appendix B1 – ethnic mix

- Appendix B2 – people data

- Appendix B3 – economy data

- Appendix B4 – election results

Appendix B1 shows the population (in millions) of each state, and breaks that number out into percentages of five self-identified ethnic categories. These five categories are (non-Hispanic) white, black or African-American, Hispanic (or Latino), Asian, and other (American Indian, Alaskan or Hawaiian native, other Pacific islander). It also shows averages for each of the nine lands and aggregate proportions for the USA. Thus, (the states making up) Progressiveland had a 2016 population of 65 million, of which 61% considered themselves to be non-Hispanic white, 15% to be African-American, and 14% to be Hispanic. The data sources are Tables 19-20 of the 2018 edition of the Statistical Abstract of the United States (developed and published by ProQuest).

Appendix B1 shows that the ethnic mix of the country is not uniform by state or region. Whites (as defined) comprise about 60% of the population countrywide, but are as high as 79% in Appalachialand (even higher in some individual states), and as low as 34% in DC and California and 15% in Hawaii. Blacks are 13% of the national population, but are as high as 23% in Dixieland, and as low as 1% in several states. Hispanics are 18% of the national population, but are as high as 49% in New Mexico and 39% in California and Texas, and as low as 2% in Vermont and West Virginia. 6% of Americans are of Asian ancestry, but Asians make up 38% of the Hawaiian population (with another 34% being Hawaiian natives or other Pacific islanders).

Appendix B2 shows state and regional miscellaneous data in six categories:

- MIGR (16) – net migration (000, 2010-2016)

- SMOK (212) – proportion of adults aged 18+ who currently smoke (%, 2015)

- EDUC (255) – proportion of adults aged 25+ years with at least a bachelor's degree (%, 2015)

- SAL$ (270) – average salary per classroom teacher ($000, 2016)

- ABOR (107) – rate of abortions per 1000 females aged 14-44 (2010)

- VIOL (334) – rate of violent crimes per 100,000 people (2015).

Parenthetical references above are to the source Table in the 2018 edition of the Statistical Abstract of the United States

Appendix B2 shows that the variations by state and region in these demographic measures are significant but not overwhelming.

Appendix B3 shows state and regional economic data in six categories:

- LABR (688) – workers covered by unions (%, 2016)

- INC$ (704) – personal income per capita ($000, 2016)

- PVTY (733) – individuals below poverty level (%, 2015)

- AGR$ (870) – value of agricultural production ($ billion, 2015)

- OILR (941) – crude oil reserves (billion barrels, 2015)

- COAL (949) – coal reserves (billion tons, 2015)

Parenthetical references above are to the source Table in the 2018 edition of the Statistical Abstract of the United States.

Appendix B3 shows clearly that, although all the new lands are viable in economic and other terms, they all will need trading partners among the other new-USA lands, and indeed among the other nations of the world.

Appendix B4 shows US Presidential election results by state for the first five elections of the 21st century, as well as the electoral votes available in each state in 2016. Electoral vote results by political party are covered in Chapter 6.

APPENDIX B1 - ETHNIC MIX OF THE UNITED STATES

STATE	POP	WHITE	BLACK	HISP	ASIAN	OTHER
CT	4	65	12	16	5	3
DE	1	61	23	9	4	3
DC	1	34	48	11	4	4
MA	7	70	9	11	7	3
MD	6	50	31	10	7	3
ME	1	93	2	2	1	2
NH	1	90	1	4	3	2
NJ	9	52	15	20	10	3
NY	20	51	18	19	9	4
PA	13	75	12	7	3	2
RI	1	70	8	15	4	4
VT	1	93	1	2	2	2
PROG	65	61	15	14	7	3
AL	5	65	27	4	1	2
FL	21	53	17	25	3	3
GA	10	52	32	9	4	3
MS	3	56	38	3	1	2
NC	10	62	22	9	3	4
SC	5	63	27	6	2	2
VA	8	61	20	9	7	4
DIXIE	62	57	23	13	3	3
IN	7	79	10	7	2	2
KY	4	84	8	4	1	2
OH	12	79	13	4	2	3
TN	7	73	17	5	2	2
WV	2	92	4	2	1	2
APPAL	32	79	12	5	2	2
IL	13	60	15	17	6	3
MI	10	75	14	5	3	3
MN	6	80	6	5	5	4
WI	6	81	7	7	3	3
UNION	35	71	12	10	4	3

APPENDIX B1 - ETHNIC MIX OF THE UNITED STATES

STATE	POP	WHITE	BLACK	HISP	ASIAN	OTHER
AR	3	72	16	7	2	3
IA	3	86	4	6	3	2
KS	3	75	6	12	3	4
LA	5	58	33	5	2	2
MO	6	79	12	4	2	3
ND	1	84	3	4	2	8
NE	2	78	5	11	2	4
OK	4	64	8	10	2	15
SD	1	81	2	4	2	11
TX	28	40	13	39	5	3
HEART	56	57	13	23	3	4
AK	1	59	4	7	6	24
AZ	7	52	5	31	3	8
CO	6	66	4	21	3	5
ID	2	81	1	12	1	4
MT	1	86	1	4	1	9
NM	2	34	3	49	2	13
NV	3	47	10	28	9	7
UT	3	77	1	14	3	5
WY	1	83	1	10	1	5
ROCKY	26	61	4	24	4	8
OR	4	75	2	13	4	6
WA	7	68	4	12	9	7
GREEN	11	70	3	13	7	7
CA	39	34	6	39	15	6
PROM	39	34	6	39	15	6
HI	1	15	2	10	38	34
FED	1	15	2	10	38	34
USA	323	59	13	18	6	4

APPENDIX B2 - MISCELLANEOUS STATE DATA - PEOPLE

STATE	MIGR	SMOK	EDUC	SAL$	ABOR	VIOL
CT	-35	14	38	72	22	219
DE	36	17	31	60	37	499
DC	50	16	57	76	29	1269
MA	163	14	42	77	18	391
MD	78	15	39	67	29	457
ME	8	20	30	51	10	130
NH	10	16	36	57	12	199
NJ	-39	14	38	69	28	255
NY	-147	15	35	79	35	380
PA	11	18	30	65	16	315
RI	-3	16	33	66	20	243
VT	-4	16	37	59	12	118
PROG	128	16	37	67	22	373
AL	28	21	24	49	11	472
FL	1562	16	28	49	24	462
GA	263	18	30	54	17	378
MS	-35	23	21	43	4	276
NC	370	19	29	48	17	347
SC	244	20	27	49	7	505
VA	158	17	37	51	17	196
DIXIE	2590	19	28	49	14	377
IN	5	21	25	51	8	388
KY	26	26	23	52	5	219
OH	-70	22	27	56	14	292
TN	191	22	26	48	14	612
WV	-10	26	20	46	7	338
APPAL	142	23	24	51	10	370
IL	-362	15	33	61	17	384
MI	-88	21	28	62	16	416
MN	42	16	35	57	11	243
WI	-20	17	28	54	7	306
UNION	-428	17	31	59	13	337

APPENDIX B2 - MISCELLANEOUS STATE DATA - PEOPLE

STATE	MIGR	SMOK	EDUC	SAL$	ABOR	VIOL
AR	22	25	22	48	8	521
IA	25	18	27	54	10	286
KS	-35	18	32	48	13	390
LA	22	22	23	50	14	540
MO	-7	22	28	48	5	497
ND	56	19	29	51	10	237
NE	15	17	30	51	7	275
OK	78	22	25	45	9	422
SD	21	20	28	42	5	383
TX	1376	15	28	52	15	412
HEART	1573	20	27	49	10	396
AK	-13	19	30	67	13	730
AZ	305	14	28	47	12	410
CO	306	16	39	46	15	321
ID	47	14	26	46	6	216
MT	34	19	31	51	12	350
NM	-38	18	27	47	14	656
NV	147	17	24	57	22	696
UT	65	9	32	47	6	236
WY	3	19	26	58	1	222
ROCKY	856	16	29	52	11	426
OR	184	17	32	60	15	260
WA	333	15	34	54	16	284
GREEN	517	16	33	57	16	272
CA	443	12	32	77	24	426
PROM	443	12	32	77	24	426
HI	20	14	31	57	21	293
FED	20	14	31	57	21	293
USA	5842	18	31	58	18	383

APPENDIX B3 - MISCELLANEOUS STATE DATA - ECONOMY

STATE	LABR	INC$	PVTY	AGR$	OILR	COAL
CT	18	71	11	1	0	0
DE	18	49	12	1	0	0
DC	11	76	17	0	0	0
MA	13	65	12	1	0	0
MD	12	58	10	3	0	1
ME	14	44	13	1	0	0
NH	11	58	8	0	0	0
NJ	17	62	11	1	0	0
NY	25	61	15	6	0	0
PA	13	51	13	9	0	26
RI	17	52	14	0	0	0
VT	13	50	10	1	0	0
PROG	15	58	12	24	0	27
AL	9	39	19	6	0	4
FL	7	46	16	9	0	0
GA	5	42	17	10	0	0
MS	8	36	22	6	0	0
NC	4	42	16	13	0	0
SC	3	39	17	3	0	0
VA	6	54	11	5	0	1
DIXIE	6	43	17	52	0	5
IN	11	43	15	12	0	9
KY	13	39	19	7	0	28
OH	14	45	15	11	0	23
TN	6	43	17	5	0	1
WV	13	37	18	1	0	30
APPAL	11	41	17	36	0	91
IL	15	52	14	17	0	104
MI	16	44	16	9	0	0
MN	15	52	10	20	0	0
WI	9	47	12	13	0	0
UNION	14	49	13	59	0	104

APPENDIX B3 - MISCELLANEOUS STATE DATA - ECONOMY

STATE	LABR	INC$	PVTY	AGR$	OILR	COAL
AR	5	39	19	10	0	0
IA	11	47	12	31	0	2
KS	10	49	13	18	0	1
LA	5	43	20	4	0	0
MO	11	44	15	11	0	6
ND	7	55	11	9	5	9
NE	9	50	13	25	0	0
OK	7	46	16	8	1	2
SD	7	48	14	11	0	0
TX	5	48	16	29	12	12
HEART	8	47	15	156	18	32
AK	20	55	10	0	2	6
AZ	6	40	17	4	0	0
CO	11	52	12	9	1	16
ID	7	39	15	8	0	0
MT	14	42	15	5	0	119
NM	8	39	20	3	1	12
NV	15	44	15	1	0	0
UT	6	41	11	2	0	5
WY	7	55	11	2	1	58
ROCKY	10	45	14	34	5	216
OR	16	45	15	6	0	0
WA	19	53	12	11	0	1
GREEN	18	49	14	17	0	1
CA	18	56	15	50	2	0
PROM	18	56	15	50	2	0
HI	21	51	11	1	0	0
FED	21	51	11	1	0	0
USA	12	50	15	429	25	477

APPENDIX B4 - PRESIDENTIAL ELECTION RESULTS (2000-16)

| STATE | REPUBLICAN % | | | | | ELEC VOTES |
	2000	2004	2008	2012	2016	
CT	38	44	38	41	41	7
DE	42	46	37	40	42	3
DC	9	9	6	7	4	3
MA	32	37	36	37	32	11
MD	40	43	36	36	34	10
ME	44	45	40	40	44	4
NH	48	49	45	46	47	4
NJ	40	46	42	41	41	14
NY	35	38	36	31	32	29
PA	46	48	44	47	49	20
RI	32	39	35	35	39	4
VT	41	39	30	31	30	3
PROG	39	42	39	38	38	112
AL	56	62	60	61	62	9
FL	49	52	48	49	49	29
GA	55	58	52	53	51	16
MS	58	59	56	55	58	6
NC	56	56	50	50	50	15
SC	57	58	54	55	55	9
VA	52	54	46	47	44	13
DIXIE	53	55	51	51	51	97
IN	57	60	49	54	57	11
KY	57	60	57	60	63	8
OH	50	51	47	48	52	18
TN	51	57	57	59	61	11
WV	52	56	56	62	69	5
APPAL	53	55	51	54	57	53
IL	43	44	37	41	39	20
MI	46	48	41	45	48	16
MN	46	48	44	45	45	10
WI	48	49	42	46	47	10
UNION	45	47	40	44	44	56

APPENDIX B4 - PRESIDENTIAL ELECTION RESULTS (2000-16)

STATE	REPUBLICAN %					ELEC VOTES
	2000	2004	2008	2012	2016	
AR	51	54	59	61	61	6
IA	47	50	44	46	51	6
KS	58	62	57	60	57	6
LA	53	57	59	58	58	8
MO	50	53	49	54	57	10
ND	61	63	53	58	63	3
NE	62	66	57	60	59	5
OK	60	66	66	67	65	7
SD	60	60	53	58	62	3
TX	59	61	55	57	52	38
HEART	56	59	55	57	56	92
AK	58	61	60	55	51	3
AZ	51	55	54	54	49	11
CO	51	52	45	46	43	9
ID	67	68	62	65	59	4
MT	58	59	50	55	56	3
NM	48	50	42	43	40	5
NV	50	50	43	46	46	6
UT	67	72	63	73	46	6
WY	69	69	65	68	67	3
ROCKY	55	57	51	53	47	50
OR	47	47	40	42	39	7
WA	45	46	40	41	37	12
GREEN	45	46	40	42	38	19
CA	42	44	37	37	32	55
PROM	42	44	37	37	32	55
HI	38	45	27	28	29	4
FED	38	45	27	28	29	4
USA	48	51	46	47	46	538

9 781936 400461